The Treasure Trove

A Collection of Prose and Poetry

Marty Aftewicz
Valerie Joan Connors
Susan Crawford
Tom Leidy
Jeremy Logan
Susan J McBreairty
Chris Negron
Richard Perreault
Clayton H Ramsey
Megan Benoit Ratcliff

Carolyn Robbins
Terry Segal
Brenda Sevcik
John Sheffield
Jan Slimming
John Tabellione
Jane Turner-Haessler
George Weinstein
Mary Wivell
Lisa Youngblood

Published on Create Space by the Atlanta Writers listed on the previous page.

Copyright @ 2016
All rights reserved.

ISBN 9781539046844

Contents

5. Foreword
    The Poem That Cannot Be Written   Megan Benoit Ratcliff

6. Acknowledgments

7. A GOOD WAY TO START
8. Coat Racks   Lisa Youngblood
23. Have Yourself a Merry Little Xmas   Richard Perreault
32. 40 Days   Jeremy Logan
39. Red Bear Sparkles   Jane Turner-Haessler

57. PERSONAL MATTERS-1
58. Grandfather's House   Valerie Joan Connors
72. The Pencil Sketch   Carolyn Robbins
73. Invisible Music   Chris Negron
88. Playing Along   Megan Benoit Ratcliff
89. Sparrow   Mary Wivell
96. Angels to the Rescue   Terry Segal

99. HUMOR-1
100. Christmas in Jacktown   Tom Leidy
106. Enjoy!   John Sheffield
108. Days of Destiny   Tom Leidy
111. Two Countries Divided by Geography   John Sheffield

115. WARRIORS
116. Wars   Susan Crawford
117. Finally a Hero   Marty Aftewicz
125. Old Soldiers Never Die…   John Tabellione
129. The Lionhearted   Clayton H. Ramsey

145. MEMOIRS
146. Maxwell's Bite   Jan Slimming
165. Local Retiree Carves a Legacy: Jack Weller aka "Mr. Chips"   John Tabellione

170. Ghost Train	John Sheffield
173. NOVEL BEGINNINGS	
174. *Aftermath* Excerpt	George Weinstein
188. Different Colors	Brenda Sevcik
203. PERSONAL MATTERS-2	
204. Good Mothers	Susan McBreairty
212. Life and Coffee Grinds	Megan Benoit Ratcliff
213. I've Lost My Mother	Terry Segal
215. Celebration Conflagration	John Sheffield
217. Fired	Terry Segal
219. OTHERWORLDLY	
220. The Story of Changing Woman	Terry Segal
228. The Dance of the Martian Dragonflies	John Sheffield
229. Under a Bucket	Carolyn Robbins
239. Turn Off the Noise	Terry Segal
241. HUMOR-2	
242. Ulysses Returned	John Sheffield
245. Corporal Punishment – A Lament	Tom Leidy
251. Dirty Dudley's	John Sheffield
253. The Gorilla	John Sheffield
255. ODDS AND ENDS	
256. Inspirations: *An Essay on Writing Creatively*	Jeremy Logan
263. The Spore Family	John Sheffield
265. Damn Marching Bands	John Sheffield
266. I Believe in Failure	Megan Benoit Ratcliff
269. Maybe It's About the Story	Megan Benoit Ratcliff

271. BIOGRAPHIES

Foreword

In *The Treasure Trove: A Collection of Prose and Poetry,* twenty writers, many of whom developed their skills in the Atlanta area, offer a fine selection of fiction, non-fiction, and poetry. Many of the pieces have won awards. This anthology follows in the footsteps of *North Point of View: Tales of Alpharetta and Beyond,* produced by 20 members of the Atlanta Writers Club in 2005. Some of the pieces are new. Others had been set aside, missing previous opportunities for publication, a demise captured in the commentary below.

The Poem That Cannot Be Written

Megan Benoit Ratcliff

The poem that cannot be written is not failure, unfinished and sitting in fragments on a too-white page. The poem that cannot be written is like the sunrise that cannot be captured by a camera's lens; a tender moment that cannot be described; a caress never felt again. The poem that cannot be written is, in part, the essence of our lives. Fragments here and there pieced together and recalled but never again whole.

Acknowledgments

The covers were produced by Terry Segal.

Preparation of this anthology was coordinated by John Sheffield with help from Jason Sheffield.

A GOOD WAY TO START

Coat Racks   Lisa Youngblood

Have Yourself a Merry Little Xmas   Richard Perreault

40 Days   Jeremy Logan

Red Bear Sparkles   Jane Turner-Haessler

Coat Racks

Lisa Youngblood

Winter 2013

My husband is snoring next to me in our bed. His snore is more of a hum than a roaring engine and I have come to think of it as white noise, the kind people pay good money to hear. It is the sound of home to me, humble and honed, and I always feel a little empty when it disappears. But time stops for no person, and it is only a matter of seconds before his nose twitches and the snoring stops.

The games begin.

Our twenty-pound Maine Coon, uncanny in his timing, jumps onto the bed and crawls on top of Robert's chest. The cat wriggles his body into a comfortable position, rears back, and butts Robert in the chin. Robert's head snaps backward into the pillow and a soft smile curls his lips. Slowly, he opens his eyes. Rufus leans in for his behind-the-ears scratch, and Robert obliges. Rufus purrs, the second sound of home for me.

"Hello, Rufus," Robert says, as he does every morning. "You are getting very fat." Rufus meows in proud agreement and stretches his neck toward me for his morning pat. I give him an extra one for good measure. He purrs even louder.

Robert wipes the sleep from his eyes and sighs. "It's time to make the donuts," he says and crawls out of bed. I want to grab him and pull him back in; I want to make this very ordinary, very habitualized moment more real than all the moments that will follow - but I don't. He will find it sentimental, and it will scare him.

Being the cook of the family, Robert decides to make ham and cheese omelets. The small TV in the kitchen is on and a woman in coiffed hair and a hideous striped dress is talking about Phil Robertson, the patriarch of Duck Dynasty. Phil recently compared homosexuality to bestiality, which has caused quite a stir. "Many viewers believe that Mr. Robertson was merely standing up for what he believes," she says, her voice suggesting clear agreement with these viewers. "These people, and there are thousands of them, believe that the station's removal of Mr. Robertson is a slight to the Christian faith." Robert seems unaware of the story as he cracks four eggs into a bowl.

"Fox News?" I ask. "Really?"

Robert smiles and pulls the cheese out of the fridge and starts to grate it.

"I never thought I'd be married to a Republican," I sigh. "I didn't even know it was possible."

Robert rolls his eyes and dices a handful of ham. "I'm fiscally conservative," he says. "I feel no need to apologize for that."

I smirk and pick up the paper. The headline is about Iraq. More soldiers have died and a former officer is being accused of defection. I set it down and watch Robert at the stove. As always, he hums while he cooks, but I do not have the sense he is actually thinking about anything. He is simply humming, which seems a remarkable state of being. But, of course, Robert is remarkable. He is an atheist, but he finds the universe magic. He believes in gay marriage and bristles at religious superiority, and yet he is a Republican. That's what's hardest for me: he is a Republican, a fact I cannot bring myself to believe. "You're not really a Republican," I say as if saying it out loud will make it true.

"I'm not a Democrat," he says and slides an omelet onto a plate and hands it to me. "And anyway, the Republicans are good at kicking Palestinian ass. That's why the Jews vote for them."

"How would you know what the Jews do?" I ask. Robert was raised nominally Jewish but never mentions it unless it is to bolster an argument, at which point one might think he is Moses' grandson.

"You wouldn't understand," he says and serves himself. "You aren't a Jew."

I don't say anything about the Christmas tree his mother puts up every year (without any objection from her husband) or about the fact that he hasn't stepped foot in a synagogue since he was twelve. Instead, I take a bite of the omelet. It is delicious. Rufus rubs against my leg, waiting for me to sneak him a bite, which I do as discretely as possible. Robert pretends not to notice.

"You know," I finally say. "I may be more Jewish than you. After all, I have never had a Christian boyfriend." I let out an exaggerated sigh. "You, on the other hand, tend toward the Christian gals."

Robert smiles. "There was that Mitchell fellow," he says. "He wasn't a Jew."

"You were the one who said we should date other people in college."

"Dumbest idea I ever had."

"Agreed. Anyway, Mitchell was just a month-long mistake. It hardly counts."

"It counts to me. I hate that guy."

"You don't even know him."

"I don't have to know him to hate him." We both laugh at the absurdity of what he has said. Laughing is the crown jewel of these days, which we both seem to realize at the same moment. We grow silent and eat our omelets under the shadow of what will one day be a memory, for him at least. It was not supposed to be this way. We found each other when we were fifteen. That was sixteen years ago, and we were supposed to quintuple that number. We were supposed to be able to say that we had been together five times longer than we had been apart. But that will not happen.

***

When he comes home from work, I know the question of my visit with Dr. Langston is heavy on his mind, but he won't ask. He understands that I will talk when I can. "That wife swap show is on tonight," he says. "You wanna watch?"

"Sure. But let's order Chinese first." We busy ourselves with menus and bargains. *If you'll split an eggroll with me, I'll get the Lo Mein. Okay, but if I am going to eat an eggroll, I don't want the*

Sweet and Sour. It's too much. We have a quick debate about soup and how well it travels, and we finally decide we don't need it. I make the call and order and then join him on the sofa. He already has the TV on and is staring at it as if he is on a sinking ship and it is the land.

"You can ask," I say. "I should have never told you you couldn't."

He mutes the television.

I grab the remote and click the TV off. "There is no reason to continue the chemo."

He shakes his head. "That's absurd," he says.

"It's the truth."

His eyes begin to race around the room as if chasing a scurrying fairy. They suddenly still. "What about that guy in California?" he pleads. "The one who does the acupuncture and waves his hands over tumors until they disappear? Why don't we try him?"

"He's not for me," I say and lean over and kiss him. That is the sign that I cannot talk anymore, and he reads it well. He opens his arms and lets me tuck in. I turn the TV back on and turn up the volume. An overweight woman with thick glasses is staring at the screen as if for effect. "I don't believe in wasting your life cleaning," she says. "It's overrated. That and the schedules and the *activities*." She says the word activities as if it is an unsavory disease. "People have just forgot how to live in the moment." The camera pans the room to reveal the hovel of a hoarder. It zooms in on a beat up pizza box sandwiched in the middle of a waist-high pile of magazines and then fades away, whereupon a new woman is on the screen. She has on a white, starched shirt and has a list in her hand. The two of them are about to swap families. "Some people say it's OCD," she snickers. "But I'd say they are just lazy. If you can't find it, you don't deserve it. If you don't want to put in the work, you may as well not exist." I pinch Robert's arm. "This is going to be a good one," I say.

He glances at me in confusion and I point to the television. "Oh," he says. "Yeah. I guess so."

Rufus meows and jumps onto the sofa. He stares at us uncertainly and then opts to lie alone at the other end. "It's okay," Robert says to Rufus. "Everything is fine."

***

I won't get out of the hospital this time, which bothers me. It's not the dying part so much (I'm used to that), it's the feeling that I failed to appreciate the things in my life, all those little objects and knick-knacks Robert and I accumulated over the years. There was a pebble we brought back from a wonderful weekend in Chicago. It had been worn down by the shores of Lake Michigan so uniquely that it appeared to bear a human face. A perfect tiny nose. Two symmetrical eyes. We had joked that on our return, we would find its torso. But we did not return – and we never will. And I want to see that rock again. I want to hold it in my hands and squeeze the life out of it. And Rufus. He'll never understand why I didn't come home. I think there should be a way to say good-bye to a cat.

Robert has not left my side. The nurses have encouraged him to go home and get some sleep but he won't listen. "They're so bossy," he complains every time one leaves the room. He is asleep now on his makeshift bed, two vinyl chairs smashed unconvincingly together, more than a little intent on separating in the middle of the night. At the moment his rear-end sags through the crevice and has forced his body into a strange V shape, which has deepened his snoring. He has become my own personal foghorn.

As I listen, I scan the room, imagining I am out at sea somewhere, maybe a cruise through the Galapagos. But the vinyl furniture and the tubes and monitors do little to sustain my fantasy, and I am catapulted back into this crappy little room. Still, there are flowers – and that's something. Robert had lilies delivered last week. Unfortunately, their perfume is slipping into putridity and the water in the vase has grown cloudy. They will have to be tossed soon. But these flowers are not just flowers, and they are certainly not just flowers that are dying. They are a gift intended to cheer me up. That is my job now. I have to be as cheerful as possible. It is the only thing I have left to offer Robert.

"Don't you ever sleep?" he asks as he struggles to extricate his rear-end from his splitting chairs. His eyes are swollen and the skin beneath them sags like shadowed waves.

"I don't like sleeping anymore," I answer honestly. "I like seeing things. And remembering."

Robert grimaces and I feel my heart race. Words have become landmines. I wait for him to stand and stretch and splash a little water on his face.

"You can turn on the news if you want," I offer. "I don't mind listening to a few Republicans touting their family values. You know, the ones that only apply to white heterosexuals. It's fascinating."

He smiles and I feel a wave of gratitude. "They're not all like that," he says. "You're being hyperbolic and stereotypical."

"*Oooh, hyperbolic*! That sounds so passionate."

He rolls his eyes and turns on the news. A red line streams across the bottom of the screen that reads: *Breaking News*. It is in all red letters but doesn't appear to me to be that urgent. Apparently, Miley Cyrus likes to twerk. That's fine by me. Last time I checked, it was still legal.

"Isn't that hideous?" says a voice from the hall. It is Mrs. Cullen, my husband's new friend. Her husband has the room across from mine, and he will not be going home either. She is trying hard to be strong but she is so pale and fragile, it is a wonder she is even standing. She often lingers at our door when she sees we are awake. I believe she is afraid of being alone, which is a problem because that is exactly where she will be in the very near future.

"Come in, Gertrude," Robert says. I feel my brow crinkle. I did not know her first name, which means he has been with her when I have been sleeping, which means he already has a life outside of me. This should be comforting, but it is not.

Mrs. Cullen comes in and accepts the seat Robert offers. "Just think about all those children who have looked up to that girl forever," she says. "What was that Disney show she was on?"

"Hannah Montana," I answer.

She nods. "Yes, Hannah Montana. And now she is behaving like a prostitute and corrupting thousands – or maybe millions – of young girls. It's shameful." She dusts off her skirt as if the mere mention of Miley has somehow soiled her.

I have a litany of responses on my tongue, but she is Robert's friend and it would be unfair to take her from him, so I keep my mouth shut. I remind myself of my job.

"It might not be as bad as all that," Robert offers. "She's just trying to grow up."

Mrs. Cullen bristles for a moment but then shrugs. "It's the parents' fault," she sighs. "It's always the parents."

She points to the television. "There he is again. Obama. Pushing the virtues of his communist healthcare plan and cramming gay marriage down our throats. Doesn't it scare you how quickly the Democrats are willing to desecrate the sacred vow of marriage?"

We all turn toward the TV. Obama is not talking about healthcare or gay marriage. He is talking about guns. "How many children have to die before we hear them cry?" he asks. I glance at Mrs. Cullen. She is unpersuaded but seems in some subtle way torn, the result of which is an end to her diatribe.

"The economy," Robert whispers to me. "That is what I cared about." *Cared.* Does this mean he no longer cares? "Gertrude," he says. "Have we lost you?"

I look back to find her slumped in her chair. Her eyes are glassy. My own heart begins to race. Robert walks over to her and grabs her hand. She takes in a startled breath and scans the room as if trying to get her bearings. Finally, her chin begins to bob.

"What is it, dear?" she asks.

"Are you all right?"

She glances at me and smiles, although the smile is a pitiful one, and suddenly her eyes harden as if she has been forced to see something she has avoided for a lifetime. "No," she says. "I am not all right. I am angry. The person I love more than any other person in the world is dying." She points to me. "And you are dying, and you are so young. I have prayed all my life, and I have been a good Christian woman. And the rest of my time on this earth is going to be hell." Robert reaches for her and she stands and lets him hold her. She is such a frail thing. She reminds me of a baby bird.

***

Days disappear and there are discussions of hospice, but there seems to be a general consensus that moving me from one spot to another is not a good use of time. The paperwork alone would likely outlast me, a fact that is utterly sobering and one which we do not discuss.

Robert seems to age by the hour. He has lost weight and his cheekbones appear to be etched from stone. His eyes are red and swollen. His hands shake. I am constantly looking away.

We have been forced to let go of many of our routines, but I have insisted we hold on to one: the news. It seems to me that if the world keeps moving, and people keep making mistakes and being brave and horrible and greedy and unbelievably generous, and I can watch, then I am still alive – still a part of the mix. This is an ironic gift to the dying: absolute clarity on the beauty of being alive, even in life's ugliest moments.

Tonight, it is Governor Christie on the hot seat. I've always liked him (even though he's a Republican), but, like everyone else, it seems he might have a vindictive streak. He has been accused of purposefully creating a horrible traffic jam out of spite. "Do you think he knew about the bridge?" I ask Robert.

Robert shrugs and lifts his rear end back through the crevice. It is a constant battle.

"If he did, and someone can prove it," I say, "then Hillary could be our next president. What do you think about them apples?"

He shudders. "Rotten," he says. "One Clinton is enough."

I feel a welcome rush of adrenaline. The rhetoric has become so soothing, so familiar, so reminiscent of a time when we thought it all mattered so much. "You're right," I snicker. "What we really need is another Bush. So articulate. So solid at policy. So economically brilliant."

Robert smiles and pushes his chairs apart so he is now sitting erect in one. He stretches and his shoulder pops. He lets out a long, low sigh. "Poppa Bear Bush was quite good," he says, "if a little less than dynamic, and Baby Bear at least managed to steer clear of blow jobs in the oval office, so he had that going for him."

I had to concede the point. Clinton, by just being his larger-than-life self, makes it hard sometimes to mount a worthy defense, and Hillary is a little harsh, a little scary. But still, they're on my team; so I defend them. This is not about being right. "She'd be a good president," I say. "She's smart and experienced and she knows how to weather the worst kind of storms."

"I don't think the women who enjoy baking cookies are going to vote for her," he says. "And there are a lot of them." He smiles at his own comment but it has sent me down a road I try never to travel: parenthood. I won't make it there. But Robert still can, and I have to let him know.

"You should have children," I say. "When I'm gone, I want you to remarry and I want you to have a child. I'm sorry we were never able to do that together."

His smile disappears and he shakes his head. He refuses to discuss his life after me, as if by so doing he can keep me here. How I wish he could – but not like this, not with tubes that feed me and relieve me and carry away all my wastes.

Governor Christie's voice grabs my attention. It crackles with anger. "There is no evidence," he spits. "Not one shred. If this is the only way David Wildstein can protect himself, then he is a coward, and, like every coward, he feeds on fabrication."

Robert is staring at the TV now. "He's pissed," he says. "Makes him believable."

I agree but I don't admit it. It's no fun to agree. And, at the moment, there are bigger fish to fry. "You don't have to say anything," I say. "But when the time comes, I want you to remember this conversation and know that it's what I want for you. You have my blessing."

His eyes are glassy. "I'm not talking about this," he says but I hope, when the time is right, he will remember that I said it. I avoid the question of whether I really mean it and settle on the reality that my best self means it – even if my whole self does not. His shoulders begin to tremble and I know I need to lighten his load. I want to be cheerful, but it is becoming farcical. What sane person would be cheerful at the door of death? "It would have been a disaster with us anyway," I say, navigating the moment in the only way I know how. "I would want the kids to be Democrats and you'd want them to be Republicans, and then we would fight all the time, and it would just be a mess."

He wipes his eyes and smiles. "Sure enough," he says.

"Yup," I continue. "Maybe you can find a sweet Tea Party Republican, and you can take family outings to abortion clinics and threaten the pregnant teenagers. That would be nice."

"We wouldn't *threaten*," he says. "We would merely *educate*." He stands and turns off the television. He sits at the foot of my bed and massages my feet through the covers. I feel my body relax until a piercing pain rips through my abdomen and sends me reeling forward. Robert grabs the morphine hose and pumps it. It floods my system and suddenly I am put in mind of a coat rack, a wooden skeleton lodged in the corner of a room meant solely to hold that which has been removed. What a seemingly useless object. It just holds coats. That's it. A coat is not a person. It is not the essence of anything. It is not even an idea.

Everything goes black.

***

The pain is bearable today. I am allowed to keep the morphine at its lowest level, which is important to me. I want to keep Robert in focus for as long as possible. He is eating breakfast, or at least trying to. He doesn't like to eat in front of me (I can't actually eat anymore), but I don't want him to leave, so he does it anyway. I am aware that it is unfair to hold him hostage and that it is at odds with my intended cheerfulness and planned graceful death, but I know now that there is no cheer or grace in death except insofar as you accept it, which I have.

Robert is moving his eggs from one side of the plate to the other like a child. "I'm not persuaded," I say. "You need to eat."

He looks up at me and smirks. "I'm not hungry." He glances across the hall. With a start, I realize Mr. Cullen's room is empty. I feel as if I am on the downward dive of a roller coaster. "He died last night," he says. "Gertrude was a mess."

I can't make myself look at him. I'm next. In a matter of days - or maybe hours - I'll be as gone as Mr. Cullen. I glance at the TV. They are still talking about Governor Christie. He looks more tired than angry today, which is even more unsettling for some reason.

"Anything new in the news?" I ask, falling back on known roads.

"A horrible ice storm in Atlanta," comes a voice from the hall. I look over to see Mrs. Cullen in the doorway. She is showered and wearing makeup. She has on a starched shirt. A shiny leather handbag dangles from her shoulder. "Thousands of people were stranded on the highways. They had to sleep there, poor souls. One woman even gave birth. Can you imagine?" I turn back to the TV and sure enough there is a picture of Interstate 285 in Atlanta. It is a parking lot of jack-knifed trucks and jumbled cars. No one is moving.

Mrs. Cullen walks in and squeezes my hand. She gives Robert a hug. He pulls a chair over to her and she takes a seat. "Of course, all they can talk about now is who is to blame, when it seems pretty obvious to me."

"Yeah, the government should have warned people," Robert agrees. "Should have staggered the exodus."

"No, dear," Mrs. Cullen says. "It was God's fault. He sent too much ice."

I glance at Robert, who looks supremely concerned. "Are you all right, Gertrude?" he asks. "You don't sound like yourself."

She shuffles in her chair and takes a deep breath. "Obamacare is a nightmare," she says. "The cost of my husband's treatment sky-rocketed when that went into effect. We could afford it, thank God, but it's going to be a death sentence for some poor soul out there."

Robert looks at me and shakes his head, almost imperceptibly but still with the obvious intent of stopping me from arguing. But I wouldn't say anything to hurt this woman – not now.

"I'm going to miss him," Mrs. Cullen says. "Every day." She looks at me as if it is very important that I hear her. "Robert will miss you, too. That's why I'm here. To tell you that. He will never forget you. You will always be alive in his thoughts." She shakes her head vehemently. "People have always said that, and I have agreed, but I didn't understand. Not really. Not until today. The only thing that is real is the people we love – whether they are walking this earth or not. Do you hear what I'm saying?"

I nod and think of my coat rack. In my mind, it is wooden and there are small cracks in its long spine, evidence of the weight it has had to bear. Pebbles from the shores of Lake Michigan. Governor Christie's jammed highways. Phil Robertson's religious zealotry and his caricatured family. Miley's twerking hips. Family values. Republicans. Democrats. They are all just coats, discarded and hanging limply in a corner – even as lights shine on them. But coats keep us warm. And sometimes that is what we need, if for no other reason than to keep us moving forward. Real or not real, they matter for the living.

I motion for Robert to take Mrs. Cullen into the hallway. She needs his expansive shoulders and I need away from the pain in her eyes. He obliges and the two walk to the cafeteria for coffee. It is over an hour before he returns. He is ashen white, and my stomach lurches. "I don't know if she is going to make it," he says. "It's like she's disappeared."

I am suddenly very cold. Chills rake through my body. I reach for what I know. "There's an election coming soon," I say. "There will be plenty of things to be outraged over. That will help."

He laughs and sits on my bed. "Did it bother you how much we disagreed?" he asks. I wonder if he knows he has used the past tense.

"No," I say. "It was fun." I'm using the past tense, too. It is time – or close enough.

He grabs my hand. I notice that I can no longer feel my legs. But I can feel my fingers and feel his interlaced with them – and I am grateful for that. "Can we agree on one thing though?" I ask, finding an odd moment of cheerfulness sneaking through the dark.

"Of course."

The numbness is travelling up my body. It reaches my waist. I lose the feeling of having a stomach. "Newt Gingrich," I say. "Can we agree that he is an idiot?"

Robert smiles. His teeth are so straight. "Absolutely not," he says. "He's brilliant. An ass maybe, but a brilliant one."

I feel myself smile.

April 2016

Robert places the bouquet of lilies on the grave and pulls a Ziploc from his pocket. The bag contains a tuft of Rufus' fur, which he blows into the wind. He takes his seat on the grass. He listens as the birds preen and prattle for mates. "I miss you," he says and rubs his hands through his hair. He brushes a few stray leaves from the base of her tombstone. "You wouldn't believe what's happening," he says. "It looks like Donald Trump is going to be the Republican nominee. *Donald Trump!*"

A squirrel races down a nearby limb and the tree shakes as if it is laughing.

"No," Robert says. "I am not kidding. But I'm still not voting for Hillary, and Bernie is a communist – so that's a no-go, too."

A car pulls into the cemetery but no one gets out. He remembers how hard it was when he first came for his visits, the reality that sunk in with each step forward. He wants to tell the person that it will get easier, but he knows better than to interfere with the progression of another's grief.

"Oh, I know," he continues. "Cruz is a fanatic, too. Evangelical. Crazy religious and unlikeable."

The car door creaks open but still no one gets out.

"We may have reached an impasse," he concedes and then laughs. "No, you'll vote for Hillary. You yellow-dog democrat."

A woman emerges from the car. She is alarmingly young. He wonders who she has lost.

"Trump wants to build a wall around Mexico," he continues. "No wait – that is what you would say. He doesn't really want to build a wall. He's just saying that to get elected. At least he knows how to run a company."

The woman is walking toward a grave on the other side of the cemetery. Her head is down and she moves gracefully but slowly. Whoever she has lost has only recently passed. His own chest tightens. It is time to say what he has come to say. "I heard you," he whispers. "And I want to thank you."

A bird lands on the tombstone but quickly flies away.

"Her name is Jennifer. She has red hair and a nice smile. She likes Chinese food, too." He takes a deep breath, satisfied in his conversation. "You would like her. I know it."

The wind seems to whisper, which makes Robert laugh. "Even better," he says. "She's a Libertarian."

Have Yourself a Merry Little

Richard Perreault

Christmas was barreling down on the little mountain town of Fruition, North Carolina like a snowball with an attitude—white and woolly, sparkling with the promise of peace on Earth and bargains at the Goodwill. Electric snowflakes the size of hay rolls hung from telephone poles, flower boxes that in warmer days boasted petunias and begonias now harbored plastic poinsettias. Since the week after Halloween, swirls of aerosol snow scrawled storefront windows wishing all who cared to have one, a *Merry X-Mas*.

On the lawn of The House of the Prayerful People Bible Chapel a moveable-letter sign proclaimed:

Merry Xmas
Jesus is the reason f r the s ason.

Next to the sign, a nativity scene presented the traditional distortion of Biblical chronology—Wise Men, shepherds, and angel in simultaneous attendance. The decades-old polyethylene Baby Jesus had been replaced with a more life-like doll, lovingly wrapped in a blue Snuggie; twenty-first century swaddling clothes. Clustered around the crèche, an unheavenly host of inflatable snowmen, reindeer, and peevish elves paid homage to the holy child.

No one could doubt the spirit of the season had enfolded the town in its arms and given it a big Christmas hug. But for Cissie Loudermilk, who believed in neither Jesus nor Santa, Christmas was just a day the liquor stores wouldn't be open.

Each year when November came off the calendar, Cissie steeled herself against the fa-la-la'ing, angel-harking season that lay ahead. Hanging on by her chewed-to-the-quick fingernails until January arrived. Not that January was anything to look forward to, but at least it was honest. Unlike December's pretense of peace and joy, January made no bones about what it held in store: cold and bleak, ushering in yet another year of loneliness and disappointment. A year where meager hopes for something better would play out like cards in a game of solitaire, one laid upon another until there was nowhere left to play.

Cissie's dislike of Christmas wasn't personal against either Jesus or Santa. As far as she could tell, Jesus was an okay kind of guy—just not *her* kind of guy. As for Santa, he was only the first of many men who'd let her down. Even as a child she'd questioned the jolly old elf's sense of fair play. While her stocking—hung by the chimney with as much care as a five-year-old could muster—yielded a package of pencils and a hair brush, her best friend Barbara Cochran's stocking was a yuletide horn of plenty. Cissie had learned early on that low expectations were far less fragile than high hopes. Though he brought little else, the fat man in the red suit had at least brought her a valuable lesson.

The Christmas propaganda of families gathering to share the joy of the season was as useless to Cissie as sunscreen on a snowman. Her mother, like Ebenezer Scrooge's partner, Jacob Marley, was dead as a doornail. Her father she had not seen in person for more than four years, though he appeared with disturbing regularity in tortured dreams from which she'd wake with clenched fists, whimpering into her pillow.

The days had counted down, flying off the calendar like Canada geese with reservations in Acapulco. Now, it was Christmas Eve, and Cissie was faced with the loneliness and gathering darkness of a frigid winter night supposed to be bright with celebration. She was going to need a friend, and the only friend she could count on was Johnny Walker.

As she pulled into the parking lot of the Red Dot, the irony of the town's only liquor store sitting adjacent to The House of the Prayerful People didn't escape her. To complete the incongruous trinity, a McDonald's had been built directly across the street from the church.

Behind the liquor store, a street lamp haloed a stand of oak trees, crowns of mistletoe dotting the highest of the otherwise naked limbs. A pagan symbol coopted in modern times to prompt public displays of affection, Cissie saw the plant as just another parasite sucking marrow from the bones of the season. Anyone bringing a cluster of the filthy stuff near her would be welcome to a kiss all right, as long as the kiss was planted firmly on her ass.

With two bottles of Johnny Walker Red tucked under the passenger seat, Cissie pointed her pearly-blue Dodge Neon toward the road leading up to Dancing Dog Ridge, a road wide enough for only a car-and-a-half, where deference was more advised than aggression.

When she'd made it to the top and parked the car, overlooking the dots of lights in the valley below, she broke the seal and unscrewed the cap from one of the bottles of scotch. She took a deep, throat-burning swig, wiped her mouth on her sleeve, and turned on the radio. To avoid the intrusion of Christmas music, she navigated quickly to a talk radio station.

What Cissie disliked most about Christmas songs were the trite, nonsensical lyrics. None of the holly-jolly, fall-in-love-in-the-snow-and-snuggle-by-the-fireplace things celebrated in the songs ever happened to her. A snowman stood a far better chance of coming to life and dancing around the town than she did of having herself a merry little Christmas.

As soon as she'd settled on a station, the national news came on. In Baltimore, a newborn baby had been stuffed into a box filled with bubble wrap and tossed into a dumpster. A house fire in a small Ohio town near Sandusky had killed at least six people. Two New York City policemen had been executed while sitting in their patrol car at an intersection in Queens, while up the river in Poughkeepsie, a violent attack at a Christmas Eve candlelight service had left eleven dead and dozens clinging to life.

Cissie turned off the radio. No matter how disconcerting her own thoughts, she preferred them to a play-by-play of the inevitable disintegration of the human race.

By the time half the scotch in the first bottle was gone, Cissie could no longer distinguish between the lights in the valley and the stars overhead. She laughed at the thought that had she been an ancient Magi following a celestial guide to the birth of a holy child, she'd have likely ended up somewhere neither wise men nor virgins were common.

She rolled the driver's window down, hoping the chill air might momentarily modulate the alcohol flowing through her body. She turned the radio on again and labored to navigate her way back down the mountain.

In Baltimore, the dumpster baby had died. The Ohio house fire toll was now seven, and the number of dead from the attack on the church in Poughkeepsie had risen to fifteen. Cissie jabbed the radio off. She gripped the steering wheel tightly with both hands, staring out into the milky pool of light her headlights were pouring into the low clinging fog. "Oh, holy effing night."

Arriving back in town, she was surprised to see the McDonald's still open. Regardless of the rhyme, reason, or lack of religious rationale for anything being open that late on Christmas Eve, a cup of coffee sounded good. She steered into the parking lot.

As she approached the door, something in the playground caught her eye. Inside the mouth of the tubular slide was what looked like a cocoon spun by a Rottweiler-size caterpillar. When she took a step closer, a man's head popped out; scruffy and furry like a giant groundhog looking to give his end of winter forecast five weeks ahead of schedule. The man crawled from the wad of blankets onto the synthetic rubber ground, looked up at Cissie and smiled. Not wanting to be caught staring, she hurried into the restaurant.

The girl behind the counter, whose nametag proclaimed her to be *MEGHAN*, appeared to be more on the *bah, humbug* side of Christmas than the *holly jolly* side. Perhaps because she was having to work on Christmas Eve.

"Can I help you?" the girl asked, still eschewing any hint of Christmas cheer.

"Just a coffee," Cissie said.

"Large?"

"Medium," Cissie said, remembering the second bottle of scotch tucked beneath the passenger seat. She wanted to be warmed inside, not jolted awake.

Meghan made change from a ten, filled a cup with coffee and handed it to Cissie, the transaction being completed without either speaking another word.

From the corner of her eye Cissie could see the cocoon man in the playground, on his knees, burrowing back into his nest in the slide. As dismal as her Christmas stood to be, at least she wouldn't be spending it inside a piece of playground apparatus.

"I hate to be a problem, but could I get another coffee?" she asked. "Maybe a large?"

"Sure," Meghan said. "You can have it for nothing. I'd like to finish this pot before I close up."

By the time Cissie got to the counter the girl had her back turned, pouring the second coffee. "While you're at it, would it be too much of a pain to get a Big Mac meal with that?"

"What they pay me for, to sell food," Meghan said. "Anything else?"

"That's all," Cissie said as she retrieved the change from her coat pocket.

She handed the money to Meghan and pushed her way outside, nudging the door open with her shoulder, a cup of coffee in each hand, the food wedged into the crook of her arm. She approached the slide and knelt beside it. "Excuse me. Sir?"

The brown cocoon stirred.

"Sir," Cissie said again.

After some ruffling of cloth and shifting about, the man's head emerged. Cissie extended the white paper bag and one of the coffees. "Not much of a Christmas Eve dinner, but it's the best I could do this time of night."

The man took the offerings, looked up at Cissie, a smile parting the whiskers at the middle of his graying beard. "Thank you," he said. "God bless you."

"God bless us everyone," Cissie said, then calling up the only other Christmassy thing she could think to say, "And to all a good night."

"To all a good night," the man said, removing the lid from his coffee, his smile again flashing from the middle of his beard.

With a coffee still in hand, Cissie crossed the street to the House of the Prayerful People. She noticed the church's sign now read:

Merry mas
the reason f r the s ason.

In the lower right hand corner, the extracted letters had been rearranged to spell *Jesis suX*.

She kicked aside a thatch of sticks to clear a space in front of the manger and sat down. She lifted the lid from the coffee and took a sip, then set the cup beside the baby and pulled the Snuggie away from its face. "Here. I forgot creamers. Hope you don't mind."

She looked again at the *Jesis suX* message at the bottom of the sign. She pulled the *i,s* and *X* from the slot and dropped them to the ground. Taking the letters she needed from the words above, she rearranged them to spell: *yea Jesus*.

"There, that's better. Isn't it?" When the baby had nothing to say, Cissie continued, "I know you're just a baby and you've probably never had coffee before." She glanced at the plastic Mary kneeling silently at the baby's side. "And your mother'd probably shoot me if she knew I gave you some—you being a newborn, and all."

Cissie lifted the cup, this time for a gulp, not a sip. "I know tomorrow's your birthday, not to mention a holiday. You'd probably planned on taking it easy. But I don't know if that's a luxury you have anymore. Have you looked around at what's going on?" She decided against telling the baby the details of the depressing news report she'd heard up on the ridge.

Overhead, the high December moon washed out every light in the sky, save a single planet—Saturn or Jupiter Cissie suspected. She tried to muster enough imagination to make the splash of light the Christmas star.

"I know we haven't had much to say to each other for awhile. That's my fault, mostly." She ran her finger around the rim of her cup. "For one thing, I'm not sure I believe you're who they say you are. Not anymore." She looked up, as if perhaps her Christmas star might guide her to the right words, as the first star purportedly guided wise men to the stable.

She looked down at the baby. "See if this makes sense to you. A loving heavenly father would love all his children the same, right? But he set things up to favor one group of them over the other. If somebody's brought up believing you're the only way to get to heaven, that's great for them, but what about the millions brought up believing something different? Being taught that something else is true and the story about you is wrong?" She touched the baby's face, tucking a stray strand of the fine synthetic hair under the Snuggie's hood. "Does that sound fair to you?" She let the coffee warm her face, wisps of steam rising like ghosts, disappearing into the darkness around her. "Doesn't sound fair to me either. Sounds like a stacked deck with one group holding all the aces. So, I don't know what to believe. All I know is you're supposed to be somebody special. If you weren't, why would so much of the world be celebrating your birthday tomorrow? And what we need right now is somebody special, to do *something*. If it's not you, then who's it going to be? Certainly not the people in charge of things. Whatever the mess, all they do is make it worse."

She took one more sip of coffee, set it beside the baby, and boosted herself to her feet.

"You go ahead and have a merry Christmas. And a happy birthday. But then, after that. Well, after that, you need to get up and get to work."

She brushed the dirt from the bottom of her slacks. "You can keep the coffee, what's left of it."

Cissie started for the road, to cross over, get in her Dodge Neon and take Johnny Walker home for a one-night stand. But when she reached the curb she stopped, turning back toward the baby.

"Look. I don't know how much help I can be. But if you think of something I can do—anything—let me know. Okay?"

Movement in the McDonald's playground caught her attention. The cocoon man, sitting astride a small plastic horse was rocking back-and-forth, waving his hand in the air like a rodeo cowboy on a Shetland pony bronco. He looked her way, raising his coffee in toast. "Merry Christmas," he shouted. "God bless us, everyone."

Cissie waved. "God bless us, everyone."

She crossed the street, fumbling with her key fob until she found the button to unlock the door. Leaning against the car, she tilted her head back, looking upward to the single bright planet overhead.

"God bless us. Everyone," she whispered, her words whitening in the cold winter air before being swallowed by the darkness.

40 Days

Jeremy Logan

My grandfather, Eugene, and his older brother were successful merchants, and once decorated Hungarian soldiers in WWI. In the 1930's, their business required that they travel around Europe and to the United States. They paid attention to the stories of German detention camps and rumors of genocide.

The danger should have been obvious. It wasn't. At least it wasn't in 1938 to their younger brother, Josef, and their good friend, Abe. They were too stubborn and trusting, believing the politicians in their homeland.But this story is not about them, it's about Gabriel and Sarah, two of their children, who were deeply in love.

Over four years, Eugene and his older brother financed the emigration of eleven families. One-by-one, the families were relocated in the United States. The brothers had the means and the determination to avoid what Germany had in mind for Jews like them. To friends and family who would listen, they offered a future of freedom if they relocated to America.

They obtained American work visas for the households that took them up on their offer. As soon as a family was rooted in New York with jobs and housing, they financed another household with the samedeal until every family household who wanted to emigrate to the U.S. was given the opportunity. Some of their Hungarian neighbors called them deserters. Were these so-called deserters foolish and paranoid? History answers that question.

Their lives in Szikszo, Hungary weren't idyllic, but tolerable, with enough opportunities for pleasure and recreation. There were plenty of anti–Semites, but they were not a threat, so long as the Jews didn't provide additional provocation for their bigotry. Starting over in the U.S. with nothing was daunting, a high stakes decision filled with uncertainty. Also, America was a place that was unfamiliar, and the claims of freedom and democracy sounded too good to be true. For many, it would be a place where they didn't know the language or had few friends and family. But the alternative was staying put, and if they chose that alternative, they might keep everything or lose everything, including their lives.

My grandparents and mother were the last Jewish family from Szikszo to make it out safely. They owned a general store that served the region, and they were wealthy compared to most of their neighbors. Their home had electricity, plumbing and phone service – a rarity. They had paid a high-ranking military official to give them a call, if and when, the Nazis came. In their attic they stored their pre-packed luggage and passports. In the seams of their packed clothes were currency and gemstones, hidden, in anticipation of the call. They did so because many migrating Jewish families were robbed as they fled to safety. The best way to retain any valuables was to wear them.

One evening, in 1938, they answered the phone and were told the day had come to flee. They had also agreed to pay a fellow merchant the equivalent of a thousand dollars to carry them to Trieste on a moment's notice. The agreement was half in advance and the rest upon their safe arrival. From there they would sail to Ellis Island in America. They were loaded onto a truck at midnight, and headed for safety.

Josef and Abe chose not to join the rest of the family and friends who were leaving for America, and stayed with their children, Gabriel and Sarah inSzikszo. My mother was fourteen, a year younger than them.

The day after my mother and grandparents fled for America, the Nazis arrived with the Hungarian Army and rounded up the Jews. Josef, Abe, and their wives were killed in their homes when they resisted. Their children fled into the woods. Gabriel and Sarah were the only children to come out of the woods alive. For three years, they wandered around Europe working for the resistance, avoiding the Nazis and battlefields. Sadly, a French traitor tipped off the German Army, and they were captured in France during a raid in 1941. They were placed in a boxcar headed to the death camps of Auschwitz and Buchenwald.

They had heard the rumors that the men would be separated from the women and sent respectively to Auschwitz and Buchenwald. Gabriel, the romantic, said to Sarah, "If we're split up we'll meet in Paris in front of the Eiffel Tower at noon. The first to arrive goes there every day until…until, you know, the other won't be arriving."

Were they foolish dreamers like their parents who believed they would be spared? What were the chances they would ever make it out alive? Zero. Young lovers are so naïve. At least Sarah had a skill. Her grandmother taught her dressmaking, and she had real talent as a seamstress. Gabriel had only meager talents. He could fight, tell stories, and he spoke French and German. Were these skills so remarkable that they could possibly save his life?

By some rare chance of luck, the commandant of Auschwitz was a boxing fan. The best fighters among the prisoners were made to fight the guards in matches arranged by his lieutenant. If the guard lost, he would be demoted. If the prisoner lost, he would be executed. But, if a prisoner won, he would get decent meals and live to fight another match in a week's time. A decent meal consisted of a potato, a green vegetable and a spoonful of protein hash that tasted awful, and was also impossible to identify. Their fear was that it was human.

Gabriel figured the only way to survive Auschwitz was to do whatever he had to do, to get decent food. He talked his way into a boxing match and won. He kept winning and became a favorite of the commandant. He was so well-liked by the commandant, that after a while, he didn't need to box or dig graves for his meals to stay alive. He became the commandant's valet, entertaining him with stories he would invent.

Sarah's fate at Buchenwald appeared to be headed in the wrong direction. She was brutally beaten by a guard when she resisted his sexual advances. She was quite attractive, and the pretty girls were raped. The rules there were very simple, obey or be beaten. And if you were beaten so badly you couldn't report for work at dawn, you'd be sent to the ovens. She was on her way to the ovens when she whispered to the head of her guard detail, "I will make your wife a fabulous gown if you spare my life."

Apparently, fine garments were quite scarce, and most of the seamstresses had been killed. He gave her a week to make his wife such a gown. She was isolated in a storage closet, but given rations, fine material, scissors, and needle and thread – nothing else but candles to illuminate the room. She succeeded and the word of her talent spread throughout the camp. Soon she was making dresses for all the German wives, including the commandant's.

Sarah and Gabriel were competitive, spirited, and as stubborn as one could imagine. Both were endowed with uncommon survival instincts. What they endured was horrific, knowing that if they did survive they would carry the scars of what they had seen and experienced the rest of their lives. Also, there was the guilt and a sense of betrayal that would come with surviving by doing what others wouldn't.

As the war wound down, the German army desperately needed fighting soldiers, not guards and attendants for the death camps. The German high command eventually drained the camps of soldiers so they could fight on the front lines. Prisoners who had the stomach, lack of conscience, or a strong will to survive were recruited to take their place.

One of the untold stories about the death camps was about Jews whose instincts drove them to do anything to survive. They were spat-upon by their fellow prisoners, who thought they had traded their souls. Those like Sarah and Gabriel had to be sequestered in separate barracks so their neighbors wouldn't kill them.

The barracks were no more than a flimsy warehouse with dirt floors, leaky roofs, and wooden bunks without mattresses. An iron stove was their only heat in the winter. They chopped their own wood for fuel, and the strongest of them got to bunk closest to the stove, given the privilege to sleep in warmth and to live another day of hard labor in the fields. The weak and least productive captives were sent to the gas chambers and ovens. Each week, another trainload of Jews arrived to take the place of those executed.

By the end of 1943, there was a crackdown on all the concentration camps. More executions had to be performed with fewer staff. Bullets and rations were scarce, needed more by soldiers on the front. The ovens worked overtime. In order to prevent disease, the Germans forced prisoners that were still living, to dig ditches to bury their dead comrades. The prisoners that were spared were given fewer and fewer rations.

By the end of 1944, many camps ceased operation, and those that were operating had little or no staff. The prisoners strong enough to dig graves were fed only potatoes and the scraps left by the rations eaten by the staff. Disease began spreading faster than the dead could be incinerated or buried. The bodies of the dead began piling up, literally creating a small mountain of human remains. When the food ran out, the living prisoners were locked in their barracks, left alone to die, as the remaining Germans abandoned their posts. Prisoners still alive were too weak and sick to try to escape. When the allied forces liberated Auschwitz, it was all but deserted, andreeking of rotting flesh.

Most prisoners found in barracks were lifeless. In building sixteen, however, Gabriel, weighing around seventy pounds, was found barely breathing. He was among a very few still alive. He was hospitalized, and when he grew strong enough to travel, he was shipped to Denmark. There he received further rehabilitation and was trained to be a policeman. After about six weeks he was free to leave to find a job, which he did--in Paris.

On the first day of duty, Gabriel ate his lunch in the shadow of the Eiffel Tower at noon. Nothing unusual happened as he silently watched the visitors, gay and fearless, pass by. After a half hour he returned to his post. That evening, sharing a hall for repatriated prisoners of war, he slept restless, haunted by nightmares of the camps. The next day he reported for work and ate another uneventful lunch at the foot of the Eiffel Tower. The next week was no different.

On the tenth day, metal park benches were installed in the plaza surrounding the Eiffel Tower. Gabriel occupied one, but no single women stopped to look around. The next day, he ate his lunch in the rain, sitting on one of the new benches. It rained again on the twelfth day, and no interesting visitors stopped to look around. And so it went for the next three weeks. After what he'd been through the last seven years, he wasn't going to allow thirty-nine uneventful days to deter him from his pledge.

The next day was a classic portrait of why young lovers visit the city. It was gloriously sunny and filled with the sounds of visitors' laughter and the aroma of meals being cooked in the fashionable restaurants. Gabriel was wondering if his bench might be too far away from the entrance to the tower. A young lady, like the one he could see passing by that very moment, might stop. But perhaps, he would go unnoticed, because he was too far away to be identified.

"I'll stand up," he said to himself. "Perhaps it will help." When he did, he saw the young woman look his way. A moment later she walked hesitantly toward him. He was still too far away to recognize anyone. He wrapped his lunch in his napkin, placed it in his pants pocket, and took a few steps in her direction. He noticed her pace quickened, and so did his. She waved her hand, and he looked nervously behind him to see if she was signaling to another. Seeing noone, he turned in her direction to see she was running.

Her hair was the right length, as was her height. Soon he was running until he collided with Sarah, the two of them collapsed on the concrete plaza in an embrace of tears and kisses.

My mother has since died at the age of seventy-seven. As I write this in 2016, Gabriel and Sarah, now in their nineties, reside in Florida. Previously, they lived in New York for fifty years, raising their children and wearing their concentration camp numbers tattooed on their forearms as if they were medals. I've heard their story told and retold many times to unbelieving listeners.

"Miracle." "Unbelievable." These are the typical responses. Their story is one of many that can be found in the holocaust museums around the world. Had I not known them, I would have been among the doubters. Instead, they are an inspiration to me. I love to hear Gabriel tell his stories and see the twinkle in Sarah's eyes as she sews. To live among them is to believe. They embody a spirit and sense of romance that simply doesn't fade.

This story is true, but I have changed the names and insignificant details so I can call it fiction. This story is really Gabriel's and Sarah's to tell, and they have where it resides in the National Holocaust Museum in Washington, D.C. It's one of enduring love, but more importantly, it is a story of survival. Elie Wiesel said: "Whoever survives a test, whatever it may be, must tell the story. That is his duty."

I have told their story here, to touch people's hearts, so that they could be inspired as I was, to retell stories worth hearing.

Red Bear Sparkles
Jane Turner-Haessler

As Mike walked through the Parkleigh Pharmacy, he felt his large six foot five body slowly crumbling beneath him. His cumbersome legs were heavy, like rotted tree trunks tied together with worn shoelaces.

He wandered into the stuffed animal section and stared blankly at the row of Teddy bears sitting together. There was a camel colored one with the standard red bow, a family of brown bears dressed in argyle sweaters, white ones, black ones and pink ones wearing ballet dresses.

It was Valentine's Day and he wanted to get a bear for Catherine, his beautiful wife of twenty-five years. The fact that it would be their last February together didn't bother him. The material world was slowly slipping away from his view, being replaced by something lighter. He made peace with God and part of him looked forward to the day he would leave his withered body behind.

It was Catherine he worried about. She didn't seem to have the strength to let him go.

He wandered into the gourmet chocolate section and gazed at all the beautiful confections under glass. Dark chocolate turtles, mocha truffles and beautifully embossed strawberry creams; they had been his favorite. If only he could still taste and feel the soft sensation of chocolate melting on his tongue.

A young woman with pale skin and a blue scarf approached him. She reminded him of his sister.

"Is there anything in particular you'd like," she asked.

"I don't know?" he said. "They all look so good. What's your favorite?"

"I don't eat chocolate," she replied. "It's bad for you."

"Really. How sad."

"There are plenty of things to eat besides chocolate," she replied, "like jelly beans."

"Jelly beans are okay, but chocolate is a heavenly delight. Do you know that people study chocolate their whole lives just to be able to create the perfect blend of flavors and texture?"

"I did not know that."

"What's your favorite flavor of Jelly beans?" he asked.

"I like strawberry."

"Very well then, I'll have a box of six strawberry creams."

"Dark chocolate or milk?"

"Dark."

She packaged them in an embossed gold box and he went over to the cashiers and paid for them. Two minutes later he was back. The young girl looked puzzled. "Could you do me a favor?" he said.

"Sure."

"Could you eat one of these chocolates and describe to me the taste."

"But, sir. I don't eat chocolate."

"Just this once. It's just…I can't taste them anymore."

She hesitated, his warm smile catching her by surprise.

"All right. Just one. I'll try just one."

"Eat it slowly," he said. "One bite at a time."

The woman bit into the candy and the instant the chocolate hit her tongue a smile spread across her face. "Wow," she said. "I've never tasted anything so perfect. I think you're right, it's heavenly."

"But what does it taste like?"

"Well… When you first bite into it you get this bitter sweet soft buttery flavor and then the sweetness of the strawberry mixes with it and it's like you're eating… warm ice cream."

Mike smiled, "Why don't you keep the whole box."

"But, I can't."

"Of course you can, it's my gift to you," he said smiling. "From heaven."

Walking out of the store into the wintery streets, soft snowflakes began to fall, lightly dusting the ground. He put his head back and let them land on his face. He laughed. He'd been alive for sixty years and never bought a box of chocolates from Parkleigh because he thought they were too expensive. Today, he didn't care.

The whiteness of the snow-covered lawns glowed against the afternoon shadows. Rochester's grey sky muted the colors around him, making him feel cold. He embraced it. It was enough to have this day and feel the crisp air against his cheeks.

His car was parked a block away but he walked in the other direction. There was no hurry, no deadlines to make, no meetings to attend. As he meandered slowly down the street he noticed things he never did before, the shape of the bushes and the way the sidewalk bowed to the right causing cracks to catch the snow as it fell. The tree that stood in front of the house on the corner looked like a blue woman reaching her arms to the sky. As he looked up, a gust of winter air almost took his breath away piercing the thick layers of his clothing. A stabbing pain ran through his entire left side. He was still alive. He stopped for a moment to gather his bones and convince them to cooperate. A bench stood five steps in front of him and he made his way over to take a seat. He gasped letting his body settle into the wood slats. His lungs screaming, he closed his eyes, felt the fullness of the day and said to himself, "This I want to remember."

      He thought of the birth of each one of his six children separately. He loved them all at first glance. Seeing their fingers and toes for the first time never got old. If God had given him twenty children he would have loved them all equally. Watching them as parents, his wife with the grandchildren, that, and Christmas service at Blessed Sacrament with the choir singing Holy Night would be what he would miss the most.

      He wondered what heaven would be like. Would he be the same person in heaven attached to the people he'd known on earth? Would he recognize Jesus? He could imagine how wonderful it must be to feel like air with no encumbrances, to have your mind set free, scattered like stars in the heavens.

      When he felt calm again he opened his eyes. There on the seat next to him sat a red teddy bear. He wondered why he hadn't noticed it before. He picked up the little bear and placed it in the light. The winter sun made it sparkle. He smiled and looked around for footprints leading to the owner of this little creature, but the sidewalk was empty. He thought of leaving the bear on the bench but as the snowfall began to increase he decided it wasn't safe. He placed the bear under his coat and made his way back to the car.

#2 Catherine

The sparkly red bear sat on the chair next to Mike's hospital bed, which took up the left corner of the dining room. The stuffed animal reminded Catherine of February, the last month when her husband had been whole. It should have represented something good and comforting but the bear made her mad. She wished Mike had never given her that stuffed creature. He had gone downhill the minute the bear had entered their house. She just wanted Mike; her best friend, to be stitched back together.

The doorbell rang and she went to let the Hospice nurse in, "How's he doing this morning?" she asked.

"The same, I think," replied Catherine. "I'm not sure he recognized me at bed time when I said good night."

"What about this morning?"

"Yes, this morning he said my name and smiled. But he's been moaning a lot. Maybe we need to up the morphine dosage again."

"Okay," replied the nurse. "And how are you doing?"

"I don't know? How should I be doing?"

"You should be a mess. I would be."

"Thanks," said Catherine. "For some reason that makes me feel better."

"I wish I could do more."

"That's enough."

The day wore on and she made an excuse to leave the house while the nurse was there. Catherine went to the grocery store even though she had no one to cook for except herself. She wandered around the store aimlessly filling the cart with food she'd probably never eat. What she really wanted to do was escape, sit in the park and smoke a pack of cigarettes. But since her husband was dying of lung cancer it seemed wrong.

She felt guilty for not having cancer when she had been a heavy smoker her entire life. She felt guilty for not wanting to stay at her husband's side but she couldn't do it. Physically he bore no resemblance to the man she had married.

He was so calm and accepting of his terrible fate she wanted to throw furniture at him, stand on the bed and curse in Polish and English. He was constantly talking to her about Gods plan and how it was his time and she had all her children to help her through this. To hell with God's plan! Why did God have to pick on her husband? A devout Catholic, he hadn't smoked a cigarette in thirty years. She couldn't even think of a single sin he'd committed in the last ten. She was the one who should be dying of cancer.

She opened the car window and lit a cigarette. Staring at the burning embers she hesitated until temptation took over. She placed the cigarette against her lips and inhaled deeply. A strange calm filled her insides, she closed her eyes and let go.

When she returned at four o'clock there was a car parked in the driveway that she didn't recognize. "Shoot!" she said to herself. "I forgot they were coming."

There had been so many visitors in and out of her house over the summer she couldn't keep track of them. Thankfully, they were a distraction. Her husband's jolly personality would magically reappear with each visit. He'd laugh and tell stories and for a brief period she'd forget that he was ill. She'd nod and smile and fake a chuckle here and there, but in reality she wasn't present. She'd float in and out of rooms serving food, answering questions. The weird thing was, that when the visitors left, she felt panic. Her husband would shrink back into a ball and return to the pain that had become his life. She'd have to help him back to bed, exhausted, slipping further away. It was as if God had tricked her into believing that her happy life was real and then returned her to the darkness she had felt as a child.

Maybe that's where he'd planned to leave her.

Maybe she deserved it.

As she entered the living room her grandson smiled with all his teeth. He ran over, and hugged her. "Grandma."

"Nate. When did you become such a man?" she said. "You're the spitting image of your father and where's that crazy mother of yours?"

"She's gone out to the car to try to find Sean's red bear."

"His red bear?"

"Yeah. It's missing again and he won't be happy 'til Mom finds it. It's like his third arm."

The door opened and her ex-daughter-in-law Mary walked in carrying a tear stained Sean. "God damn it!" Mary exclaimed. "He must have left it in the motel."

"Nice to see you too," she said.

"Sorry, I didn't mean to curse."

"Wouldn't be the first time… Sean has gotten so big."

"No kidding," replied Mary, plopping him back down on the floor.

Sean burst into tears again, held onto her leg and then threw himself down in the middle of the carpet. "What's going to happen to my red bear? He'll be all alone. He hates being alone."

Catherine smiled and put her hand on Sean's shoulder. "Your Mom will find red bear. He probably decided to spend another night at the hotel. They'll take care of him."

Sean opened one eye and then started crying again.

"Sean!" said Nate. "Red bears not dead."

"Just leave him there," said Mary. "Maybe he'll cry himself to sleep."

As Sean's sobs reverted to whimpers, the conversation lagged, filled with uncomfortable silences because they all knew they were only there for one reason; to say good bye to Mike, the grandfather, the father-in-law.

Catherine led them into the kitchen, prepared tea and they eventually made their way over to the dining room.

"Do you think he knows we're here?" said Nate.

"He knows. He's just on a lot of morphine so he goes in and out. He'll wake up in a little bit if you wait long enough."

The three of them stood quietly and, like magic, his eyes opened. "Hello," he said, smiling. "Nate where's your little brother? How about a hug."

"Be careful," said Catherine. "You don't want to strain yourself. Remember what the doctor said."

"Yes dear," he replied.

As she watched the three of them exchange conversation from the corner of the room she could hear the tremor in their voices. Then it started. Her husband rolled backwards onto the bed and cried out. "Are you all right Poppy," asked Nate. But he didn't answer.

Mary backed away from the bed and tears rolled down her cheeks.

"He's okay. Probably just a little muscle spasm." yelled Catherine running to his side. "What do you need honey? Just tell me."

The nurse came back into the room and stood quietly for a moment. "Why don't you let me take care of it," she said softly.

Everyone backed away and moved into the living room. Not a word was said. They took their places on the couch and stared at their shoes.

As soon as Sean saw he had an audience he grabbed a bell off the shelf in the corner and started ringing it. Catherine looked annoyed and then walked over to where Sean was standing, "These are my special bells," she said. "You have to be careful with them."

Sean put the bell back on the shelf and then twisted his lip. "Can I ring one of the bells?" he asked.

"You can ring this copper one," she said taking it off the shelf and handing it to him.

"Can I ring this one?" he said grabbing the glass one.

"No, no, Sean. That one's very delicate."

"What about this one," he said grabbing a gold colored one.

Before she gave him permission Sean shook the bell as loudly as he could. Catherine rolled her eyes. "What a lovely sound…" she said.

Sean quickly became bored when she didn't get angry. He ran into the dining room. "Mom!" he yelled. "It's Red Bear's brother. Can I have Red Bear's brother?"

He picked up the bear and ran into the living room parading the bear in front of them. "It's not yours Sean," said Mary. "Put it back. You can't take things that don't belong to you."

"That's all right," said Catherine brightly. "I think Sean should have Red Bear's brother. Maybe he'll help him find the other Red Bear."

"Really, he'll be fine. You don't have to give him your bear."

"Yeah," said Nate. "Sean has loads of stuffed animals at home. He's acting like a spoiled brat."

"Mary. I want him to have the bear. He's my grandchild, not a brat. And you know in my house, what I say is the law."

"I do," replied Mary. "I know when I'm licked."

"Yeah!" yelled Sean dancing around the room. "Red Bear has a brother, Red Bear has a brother…"

"Oh, jeeze," sighed Nate.

#3 Mary

As Mary cleaned her teenage son, Sean's, room, getting rid of all his childhood tokens when she found the sparkly red bear. She picked him up and was amazed at how new he still looked. Mary thought of that day. When she had hugged Mike for the last time, his body had crumpled in her arms, so little of him remained. It was strange to find the red bear on this day in February. The day she had just found out that her ex-husband's twin sister, Sara, was not going to make it.

After talking to her ex-husband, Dan, she had called his other sister to find out the details of Sara's condition. Of course it was worse than Dan suspected. He had a way of hiding the truth from himself. Cancer had taken his father, his sister Lori and now his twin. It was slowly devouring his family one by one. There had to be a strained voice in the back of his head warning him that he could be next.

Mary didn't know how Dan's mother, Catherine, was still sane. Every time another family member was diagnosed with the disease Mary felt worse than the time before. Logically it should have become easier, but watching the pain and slow disintegration of another person was horrible. And really how was she, Mary, to even comprehend what these people were going through. She was a just a bystander, on the outside looking in. Sometimes she felt like a big fat phony sending gift packages and asking them how they were feeling.

Cancer's victims started out so resolute and strong, surviving chemo and radiation. Then, after they were tortured, they'd be old, "Sorry, there's nothing we can do."

You could pray with a thousand people, scream "No" with all your might, march fifty miles wearing pink. None of it mattered. You lose, cancer wins. Cancer was a fucking serial killer.

Experience had taught Mary one thing: Never cry in front of cancers latest victim. It was important to make your visits happy occasions, for their sake, they were in enough pain. Listen to what they have to say and don't be shocked if they want to talk about dying. They know it and you know it. It's staring them in the face.

Mary decided it was time to send sparkly red bear back to his original family. He would make a perfect Valentine's gift for Sara. As she stared at the fuzzy red creature, tears gathered in the corners of her eyes. They let loose and streamed down her face. She had felt unusually close to Sara during her ordeal and the strange thing was that they'd only recently become friends, ever since she moved to Florida. They corresponded through humorous emails and texts; pretending that time was on their side.

This cancer had also precipitated a strange closeness between Mary and Dan. It was the coming of age of their shared son Nate that sparked even more feelings. He'd had become so much like his father that it was hard to love one without loving the other. It didn't diminish her love for her present husband because the son they shared was also exactly like his father. But all these feelings whirling around inside of Mary made her feel vulnerable and unsteady. She had always been the tough, resolute tower of strength who could handle anything that came her way. Now she was crying about a stupid bear.

Mary found a red piece of paper and cut out a large heart. She sat for about ten minutes going over things in her head that she could write to Sara. She didn't want to be too sloppy, too emotional or too flip. In the end she just told red bears story. Chances were Sara already knew, because one of the sisters had made it known to Mary that sparkly red bear had been their father's last gift to their mother. If one sister knew they all knew.

As she put the bear into a box a seventeen-year-old Sean came downstairs. "Wow! Mom where did you find that old bear?"

"In your closet next to the original red bear. I'm sending it to Sara for Valentine's. You don't mind do you?"

"Why would I care?"

"Because you used to think he was your red bears brother."

"Okayyy…. Whatever Mom. I think that was when I was four years old."

#4 Sara

The package arrived at Sara's house on Valentine's Day. Her husband John brought it in that morning and placed it on the coffee table in front of the lounge chair that had become her bed. She didn't open it right away because she was tired and moving too much made the pain worse. If she stayed in one place the morphine that was being pumped into her body made her feel light and the rest of the world disappeared into the background. So many random thoughts were racing through her brain that her past and present life came together in a clear pattern. But whenever she tried to open her mouth and explain this to the people she loved, it made no sense. Sometimes she believed she had said an entire sentence and then realized only one word had been spoken.

At night when she slept she caught glimpses of heaven, familiar voices sounded in the distance, beckoning her forward. She didn't tell her family about her dreams because she knew it would upset them and they wouldn't understand the peace it gave her. Just a little more time, she thought, just a few more moments with my girls and John.

Her mouth was dry and she had a sudden urge to pee. "God!" she said out loud. "Why now."

It took all her strength to push herself out of the lounger and walk four steps to the potty chair. When she had arranged herself in the chair she realized that her pants were still on. At first this made her mad. Who was this 50 year-old woman who had to use a goddamn potty chair? Then she started to laugh. If John could see her now he'd realize why she thought it was funny. She was glad he was the father of her children and the person she chose to spend her life with. She knew that when she was gone he'd be strong enough to take care of her girls.

After the ten-minute bathroom fiasco she managed to get herself a glass of water and walk back over to her lounge chair. As she sank back into the cushions she realized she'd forgotten about her pain. That's what it would feel like in heaven. A tear ran down her cheek and then she said out loud, "I'm sorry I want to go. It doesn't mean I don't love you. I just…"

As she sat in the room alone she cried for all that she was leaving behind. She cried for her children, her husband, her mother, brother, sisters, friends, even her dog. She cried until there were no tears left.

The soft chair cradled her fragile body as she leaned back, closing her eyes, and pushed a button dispersing morphine into her blood stream. A cool sensation spread across her chest and she sighed.

An hour later she opened her eyes and the first thing she saw was the box on the table. She smiled and leaned over to open it. Her fingers weren't cooperating so she ripped the packaging with her teeth. The paper fell to the floor, revealing a shoebox. Shoes, she thought. Must be a joke.

She opened the box to reveal a red paper heart. She picked it up and tried to read it, but she couldn't focus. She placed the heart on the table and pulled out sparkly red bear. She stared at it for a moment before she realized it was her father's last Valentine's gift.

She closed her eyes and a flood of childhood memories filled her head. She saw all her brothers and sisters gathered around the table eating dinner in their old house. She could smell the kielbasas and pierogi's. The voices of all her siblings played like a familiar song. Her father was seated at the head of the table smiling at all the commotion. Mom was yelling something from the kitchen as her twin brother Dan pinched her under the table. She could see the snow outside the picture window in the dining room as if it were today. If she could just stay here in this moment, everything would be right.

When she opened her eyes her father was standing right next to her. He was just as she remembered, tall, strong with a thick head of white hair and a beard. He didn't say anything but the look on his face was so warm and peaceful she wasn't afraid. He picked up the red bear, smiled, placed it on the chair and took hold of her hand.

#5 John

John had not slept in three days. He knew that Sara's time was coming to an end and the thought of not being next to her when she passed was driving him crazy. In the back of his head he had this beautiful image of her looking deep into his eyes and conveying everything they had meant to each other. It was something like the look Bogart gave to Bergman in the final scene of Casa Blanca. At the same time he was scared that the moment she died he would shatter like glass and be unable to put himself back together. He would lose his faith in God and become useless to his daughters. He would become the kind of person he couldn't live with.

As the news spread that Sara's clock was winding down the house had been filled with friends and family. Her twin brother Dan and his son had come for a visit, followed by her Mom and sister Liz who were still there. They'd made things easier but at the same time it became apparent that Sara was going sooner than he expected. He could no longer convince himself that she had another couple months or a week or even that many more days. He was helpless, living a dream, floating from one moment to the next, waiting for the floor to collapse beneath his feet.

It was a Thursday night and he only knew what day it was because he had to take out the garbage. Liz had made dinner and they had gathered around the kitchen table talking about old times while Sara dozed in her easy chair. "I couldn't get her to eat any lunch today," said Liz.

"She'll eat if she's hungry," said Catherine.

"That's true," said John. "She ate that frozen custard they sent her last night."

"Yeah," said Liz. "It always was her favorite."

The night lagged on and John was so tired he went to his room earlier than usual. Finally, around eleven o'clock, after his third beer he dozed off. He awoke at three A.M. in a panic. He sat up and tried to practice his breathing exercises.

Then he thought, "Screw this."

He walked into the family room to see how Sara was doing. Nothing looked any different. She was sleeping in the chair with the red bear in her lap and it was obvious that she was still breathing. But still he could not shake this feeling of dread. He grabbed a beer from the fridge and sat down on the couch to the left of his wife. He sat there watching her thinking how beautiful she looked with a crew cut. He thought of the stupid fight he'd had with her three months ago when she decided to stop the Chemo. Did any of it really matter? Nothing in this life was permanent. Whether she left today or two weeks from now didn't change anything.

He looked down at his hands clutching the beer bottle. They looked so old and tired. Time was so short he'd be right there in heaven with Sara, before he could blink.

When he looked up Sara was standing in front of him, her long blonde hair cascading across her shoulders. Soft music was playing in the background. Before he could say a single word she took the bottle out of his hand and placed it on the table. She took his hands in hers, leaned her head on his shoulder and they started to dance. His heart raced and yesterday became today. He looked up and saw himself in those warm eyes he had loved all these years. Time slowed and the music played continuously. Somewhere in the universe their love was just beginning and this same dance repeated over and over again. He held her close and decided he would never let her go.

Friday morning Catherine awoke to the sound of rain. She put on her slippers and walked into the kitchen to start a pot of coffee. She then walked into the family room to check on Sara. John was asleep on the sofa clutching the sparkly red bear. She walked over to her daughter and placed her hand on her forehead. It was at that moment she realized her daughter had passed.

She kissed her on the forehead and said, "Good-bye my love."

PERSONAL MATTERS-1

Grandfather's House	Valerie Joan Connors
The Pencil Sketch	Carolyn Robbins
Invisible Music	Chris Negron
Playing Along	Megan Benoit Ratcliff
Sparrow	Mary Wivell
Angels to the Rescue	Terry Segal

Grandfather's House

By Valerie Joan Connors

The property is deserted when I arrive. When I open my car window to take in the fresh air, I am amazed at how quiet it is. No sirens or traffic noise. The sunbaked ruts in the red clay driveway are so thick with weeds that I leave my car the distance of a full city block from the house and walk the rest of the way. When my aunt Margaret called to tell me that my grandfather passed away and left the property to me, I recalled a place I hadn't seen since my early childhood. It had been lovely then, filled with the sounds of family and the smell of food cooking in the kitchen. I remembered the ivory porches, decorated with scrolls and pillars that made me think of frosting on a wedding cake. And I remembered my grandmother calling to us from the second story balcony when it was time to come inside for the night.

 Now the property is overgrown, having been neglected for the decade since my grandmother's death, when my grandfather stopped caring about everything. Now the paint is chipped and stained on boards that were once smooth as silk, crisp, and welcoming. The wheelchair ramp at the side entrance must have been built for my grandmother when her health had deteriorated so much that she couldn't get around on her own anymore. By then, my grandfather would have been too old to carry her up and down the stairs.

 The last time I visited this house was when my uncle Robert got married. I was only ten years old. The long driveway had been lined with cars on both sides, and the field nearest the house had become a parking lot with uneven rows. The pillars that lined the porches on the front and side of the house had been wrapped from top to bottom with garlands made from yellow and white roses, threaded with ivy and baby's breath. Robert and Stephanie had arrived in a rented limousine, and as they approached the house I remember Stephanie's dress with its many layers rustling in the breeze, her hand securing the veil to her head for fear the wind would take it.

All the flower arrangements had been brought from the church. They seemed to cover every surface in the house, except where trays of food had been placed, or bottles of Champagne sat in huge ice buckets, waiting to be opened. When I think of that day, I remember a sky that had been a brilliant blue, the dogwood trees covered with spring blossoms as if they were dressed for a wedding, too.

Today, the sky is gray. The November breeze carries a chill that promises colder days are coming, and makes me wish I hadn't left my sweater in the car. The delicate branches of the dogwood trees are bare now, but the towering cedars wrap the house with a wall of green on three sides, as if to shelter the wooden structure from the elements, or outsiders. The roof has some shingles missing, and rust streaks descend from the widow's walk at the apex of the house like a trail of tears. All the colors I remember are gone now.

I realize I'm stalling, afraid to go inside, but I don't know why. My grandfather's illness took him from this house several years ago, when he got sick. It wasn't as if his death had occurred inside the house, but according to my one remaining relative, it hasn't been touched since the day they took him away in the ambulance. A week later he had been moved into a nursing home up in Atlanta where he spent the next three years waiting to die. Then, just for an instant, I had a glimpse of his old Irish setter, Blaze, sitting on the front porch at the top of the steps, an unfaltering sentinel who greeted each guest with either a wagging tail, or bared teeth, as he announced their arrival.

As I make my way up to the front of the house and climb the stairs to the porch, I notice that a family of bats has made its home high up in one corner. Now I want to go inside. Quickly. My hands shake as I try my key in the lock. For a moment I can't make it turn. I imagine getting in my car and driving back to New York, thinking that maybe it isn't too late to get my old job back, and wondering if moving to South Georgia was a really bad idea.

I've come this far, I tell myself. The least I can do is take a look around. I turn the key and open the door. The house smells old and musty, the light fixtures, furniture, and doorways draped in cobwebs. Everything is in shadow. The old lace curtains diffuse what little afternoon light gets in through the old, dirty windows. I try to open one of them, but find it has been painted shut, so I take a metal nail file from my purse and manage to carefully break the paint seal without doing too much damage to the window frame. The fresh air is wonderful, as I work my way around the living room and parlor, sliding the curtains apart, and raising the windows as far as I can make them go. The breeze makes dust clouds as it enters the rooms that have been closed up and still for so long.

I hold my breath as I reach for the light switch. The power company told me yesterday that service had been reinstated and that I'll have lights today, and the gas company will send someone tomorrow to light the pilot lights on the stove, the furnace, and the water heater. I wonder what I was thinking when I decided to spend the night in the house without first spending a week or two cleaning it up. I'm grateful for the space heater, air mattress, and clean sheets in the trunk of my car, but still can't imagine spending the night here. I comfort myself with the thought of the Holiday Inn I noticed on my way through the tiny town, and reserve the right to go back there and get a room for the night.

The living room and parlor at the front of the house are uncluttered. Except for the dust and cobwebs, the rooms are spotless. A coffee table book with photographs of Frank Lloyd Wright houses sits in the center of the coffee table, an empty ashtray beside it. The book reminds me that my grandfather was an architect, and that he designed this house himself. The lace-covered end table next to the overstuffed chair in the parlor holds my grandmother's glasses, her crochet hook, and a ball of pink yarn, and I wonder what she had planned to make with it, and for whom.

It's late afternoon. The sun is behind the house where there are fewer windows and little light gets in. I turn on the ceiling light in every room as I wander through the main floor of the house, but it's that time of the day when overhead lights don't seem to do any good. It's still too bright inside the house for the lights to provide warmth, and too dark to feel welcoming.

The kitchen is the only room on the main floor of the house that offers evidence of someone having lived here. Newspapers and junk mail are stacked neatly on the corner of the countertop. Then I notice one coffee cup, one plate, and two pieces of silverware in the sink, and a rush of sadness washes over me. In the final years of his life, my grandfather had been utterly, completely, and outrageously alone. I'm furious with myself for having been so wrapped up in my own life that I never took the time to come back to this place and spend time with my grandparents. And one by one, they had disappeared from this house as if they'd never been here at all. While I traveled the world, looking for a place that felt like home, my family dwindled to just Aunt Margaret and me. All I have to remind me of them is this single piece of architecture and the ghosts who live inside.

I feel a warm breeze behind me, and turn to see my grandmother at the stove, her apron tied tightly at her waist. I smell the delicious aroma of apple pie baking in the oven. She turns and smiles at me, just for an instant, and then the apparition is gone. Someone has cleaned out the refrigerator and pantry, because both are empty, and I remember something Margaret said when she called to tell me about Grandfather. Before he was moved to the nursing home, there was a neighbor who brought him food and checked up on him every day or two. She was the one who called the ambulance that took my grandfather away from this place forever.

Soon it will be dark, and I have to make a decision about where I plan to sleep tonight. So although I'm apprehensive, I decide to check out the upstairs and see if there's a bedroom that's habitable. When I'm half way up the stairs my cell phone rings and startles me so much I have to grab the railing to keep from falling back down. The man from the gas company reminds me he will be here first thing in the morning and will need access to the house.

At the top of the stairs I walk into the bathroom. The toilet bowl is empty and dry. The claw foot bathtub has rust all the way around the edge of the drain, and the rubber stopper on its beaded chain hangs from beneath the spout. When I turn the water on in the sink, the faucet sputters and spits dark brown water. I leave it running until it finally becomes clear and cold. No hot water until tomorrow. I flush the toilet four times in a row before I'm comfortable using it for the first time. The bottled water and non-perishable food I've packed in my car will hold me until morning. Tomorrow I can go into town for supplies. It will be just like camping, I tell myself.

There are six bedrooms upstairs, including the one where my grandparents slept, and I imagine my grandfather slowly climbing up the stairs, well into his nineties, and think it's a miracle he didn't tumble to his death. Then I remember the back stairs, the ones that come up from the kitchen. Aunt Margaret told me that my grandparents had installed a lift, back when my great-grandmother lived here. I realize that must be how my grandmother was able to sleep upstairs after she was confined to her wheelchair, because there are no bedrooms on the ground floor.

One by one I enter the upstairs rooms. Each of them is spotless, except for the cobwebs and dust. The beds are made and covered with quilts, extra blankets folded neatly at the foot of each one. I turn on the overhead lights as I enter each of the rooms, hoping to chase away some of the shadows, though with little luck. Many of the light bulbs refuse to work. Again, I open the windows, knowing that if I don't close them all in the next hour or two the house will soon be too cold. I take my time, looking in closets and dresser drawers, and find them all empty. By the looks of things, my grandfather had taken care to make the house ready to sell, assuming that as his only living grandchild, I would probably not consider living here. My Aunt Margaret, Grandfather's youngest sister, and my only other living relative, has no interest in leaving her home in Florida. But as the minutes pass by, and then the hours, I find myself warming to the idea that this could be my home.

I try to imagine how I will fill all of these rooms. They are all furnished, but empty of people. I think about renting out rooms, or adopting half a dozen children, then laugh out loud at both ideas. Not likely, I think. Half a dozen dogs, perhaps, even a horse or two. That's more likely. I smile, thinking about it. God knows whether I can get cable out here, and Wi-Fi. My freelance work should provide enough money to pay the taxes on the house. It's too soon for me to retire right now, but in a few more years I'll be able to start taking distributions from my 401(k), which is in pretty good shape thanks to all those years of thankless drudgery in corporate America. Now I realize that it was during all those years of six-day workweeks, twelve-hour workdays, and constant business travel, that I had stopped spending time with my family. I had let them all slip away. And I had missed my window of opportunity for having any children of my own.

I was stalling again, staring out the window of the second to last bedroom, but this time I knew why. The only room I had yet to visit was my grandparents' bedroom. My grandfather had been living alone for a long time, and he had been ill when the ambulance came to take him away. He wouldn't have had time to clean things up in there, like he'd done in the rest of the rooms. Every wall in the house needed a coat of paint, the predominant color throughout appearing to be gray. But with all the shadows and dark, empty corners of the house, I fear entering that last room most of all.

As I reach for the glass doorknob above the skeleton key hole, I take a deep breath, prepared for the worst. When I open the door to my grandfather's bedroom, much to my surprise, it's as if the sun has come out from behind a cloud. The walls are painted a warm shade of peach above the white enamel chair rail, and covered with deep floral wallpaper below. The brass bed is old, but has beautiful detail, and the bed is covered with a rich burgundy comforter. Someone must have made the bed, because it is neat and tidy, the throw pillows carefully arranged against the headboard. The dressers and night tables are covered with pictures in brass and silver frames that sit on top of handmade lace. The drawers in the highboy dresser are filled with my grandfather's clothes. I feel a chill as I slide open the top drawer of the lower, wider dresser and for a moment I glimpse a figure in the mirror, standing behind me. I blink, and focus my gaze into the mirror, but the figure is gone. When I look into the drawer, I see my grandmother's lingerie, her pastel colored gloves, and lace slips.

The two closet doors, his and hers, are both closed. I know that when I open them I will find they both are filled. Behind the first door I find my grandfather's suits, white shirts, yellowing with age, and his shoes lined up neatly on the closet floor. Inside the other closet I find dresses of every color, some mid-calf length, some longer. On the shelf above the clothing rod are hatboxes and shoe boxes stacked nearly to the ceiling.

The overstuffed chair in the corner of the room is draped with a woman's satin robe, and the nightstand on that side of the bed holds *The Complete Poems of Emily Dickenson* and a pair of reading glasses. On the side of the bed where my grandfather obviously slept, are prescription bottles and an empty drinking glass on the nightstand. These are the only signs in the room that even hint at illness or frailty. Beyond that, it looks as though both inhabitants will surely return at the end of the day and sleep in this bed.

I'm startled when I hear a woman's voice downstairs.

"Anybody home?" she calls up from the bottom of the stairs.

"I'm up here," I say, hurrying to the landing.

I see her standing there, tiny and white haired, a basket in the crook of each of her arms.

"Here," I say, hurrying down the stairs. "Those look heavy. Let me help you."

She lets me take the baskets from her, and they really *are* heavy. I'm amazed that this tiny woman has carried them, and wonder how far.

"I'm Alice," I say. "Alice Henderson. This was my grandfather's house."

"Pleased to meet you," she says, in her South Georgia accent that makes me think of summertime, magnolia trees, and a peaceful way of life. "I knew your grandfather," she says. "My name is Delilah Whitaker. I thought you could use some food. It will take a while for the refrigerator to cool down, if it even works anymore, so I brought you a few things to get you through the first night."

I have no idea who this woman is, except that she obviously was a friend of my grandfather's.

"I'm pleased to meet you, Mrs. Whitaker," I say. "But how did you know I was coming?"

"It's a small town, Alice dear," she says, unloading things from what appear to be two bottomless baskets. "My grandson, Bobby, works at the gas company. He told me you'd be arriving today."

After years in New York, I'd forgotten what life in a small town was like. Not that I have any secrets, really, but I'm going to have to start being more careful about what I do and say if news travels this fast.

"How long did you know my grandfather?" I ask.

"Oh, I knew Emmett for a very long time. We grew up together. We were high school sweethearts. Your grandfather took me to the prom."

This was news to me. I assumed he'd taken my grandmother.

"Do you live nearby?" I ask, not noticing a car outside in the driveway.

"It's not far," she says. "I live just down the road, where it bends back toward town."

"You walked all the way, carrying all this food?"

"Heavens, no," she says. "I drove my grandson's pickup truck. It's the only way to make it up to the house. I'm parked out back, that's why you can't see it through the window."

"I know what you mean," I say. "The driveway is a mess. I'm sure you saw my car out there. I was afraid I'd get a flat tire, the way I was bouncing all over the place, even going really slow."

"Don't worry," she says. "I'll have my hired man come over and see about the driveway."

"You have a hired man?" I ask, thinking I'd fallen into a scene from *Gone With the Wind* or something.

"Sorry," she says. "I'm old, and I've spent my whole life deep in the South. I suppose you'd call him a handyman now days. He's been taking care of my house, since my husband died twenty years ago. He weeds the garden, and does whatever else I need him to do. I've known his mother for years. I'm sure he'd be happy to help you out. That is, if you plan to stay here."

"I haven't decided yet," I say. "But this place is growing on me. So are you the friend who looked out for my grandfather after my grandmother died?"

"Yes, that's me," she says, in a wistful voice, her eyes becoming moist.

"I'm sorry," I say. "Where are my manners? I guess I've been in New York too long. Please, sit down."

I open a folded up cloth that holds a loaf of the finest smelling banana bread ever, and find a knife in the drawer to slice it with. We sit at the kitchen table, eating banana bread, while Delilah Whitaker tells me about the last decade and a half since my grandmother's death. I am beginning to think that Mrs. Whitaker was much more than a friend of my grandfather's.

"Now I'm the one forgetting my manners," Delilah says. "I'm sure you need to get settled in for the night, and here I am going on about your grandfather."

"It's fine," I say. "I'm learning things about my grandfather I never suspected."

"I can't help it," she says. "I believe that I loved your grandfather ever since I was ten years old. I thought we'd get married when he came home from the war. But he came back married to your grandmother, who was already pregnant with your father."

"That must have been awful for you," I say, knowing all too well how awful something like that feels.

"Yes, I suppose it was. But over the years I became friends with your grandma. When she got sick, she made me promise that I'd take care of your grandfather after she was gone. Of course I was glad to make that promise. The truth is, I always thought Emmett and I would get together for real, one day. It was a crazy idea, perhaps, but I guess I never got over him."

I'm not sure I want to know, but I can't stop myself.

"So did you?" I ask. "Get together, I mean."

"That's the sad part," she says. "He wasn't the same after she was gone. I liked to think that he married your grandma because she was pregnant and he wanted to do the right thing. But the truth is, she was the love of his life."

"I'm glad you took care of him, Delilah," I say. "He would have been completely alone, if not for you."

"We took care of each other," she says. "Maybe not the way I'd imagined it, but we were good friends. Now I'm going to let you get back to settling in. I have a million stories about Emmett that I'd love to tell you, but let's save them for next time. Will you be all right? Do you have everything you need?"

"I'll be fine," I say. "Thank you for bringing all this wonderful food."

I walk Delilah to the door, but I stop her before she reaches the bottom of the porch steps.

"Will you visit me again?" I ask.

"Of course, child," she says. "I'll drop in from time to time. I put my phone number on a piece of paper tucked inside one of those baskets. Call me any time you want company. I don't go out much, except for church on Sunday, so you'll usually find me at home."

After Delilah is gone, I walk outside and down the rutted driveway to get the clean sheets, space heater, and the smaller of my suitcases out of the car. It's nearly dark as I climb the porch stairs and go back inside the house. Now the lights make the rooms look cozy. Still, I wish I had thought to bring a portable television so I could hear some human voices. It's so quiet in the house.

In the kitchen, I make sure the refrigerator is working, and put some bottled water inside, along with the cheese and the beef sausage I found in one of Delilah's baskets. Then I climb the stairs to my grandparents' bedroom, change the sheets, and get ready for bed. I'm exhausted from the driving, the emotion of the day, and the effort of changing my life in every way. I think about what I'll do tomorrow, and decide the first thing I'm going to do is get a dog, for protection when I'm alone, but mostly for company. I begin to think about what kind of dog I want, a puppy or a little older dog that's housebroken, long hair or short, big or small. Maybe I'll get another dog just like Blaze. Before I know it, I'm sound asleep.

I wake to the sound of an unfamiliar doorbell. I've slept in sweatpants and a long sleeved tee shirt, so I'm practically dressed already. But I grab my sweatshirt off the chair and put it on to conceal the fact I'm not wearing a bra, and hurry downstairs to greet the man from the gas company.

"Good morning ma'am," he says. "I'm Bobby Whitaker from the gas company. I've come to see if I can get your pilot lights started."

"Come on in," I say. "I'm Alice Henderson."

"Yes, I know," he says. "Your grandfather was a very nice man. I knew him all my life. I was sad to learn he'd passed."

"Me too," I say. "But I hadn't seen him for a long time. I guess I got wrapped up in my own life and let him slip away from me. You're right, though. He was a really nice man. It was so good of your grandmother to look after him before he went to the nursing home."

Bobby has reached inside the hall closet where the water heater is, trying to get the pilot light lit, and he turns to look at me, confused.

"What was that?" he asks.

"Your grandmother," I say. "She said that they were good friends, especially after he was alone here."

"When did you talk to my grandmother?" he asks.

"Delilah was here yesterday," I say. "She came over to welcome me. She brought two huge baskets of food. I sure didn't have any neighbors like her in New York. We had a lovely visit."

Now Bobby is looking at me as though I've lost my mind, but I don't know why.

"There must be a mistake," he says. "You must be talking about my mother, Sarah Whitaker. She lives right down the road."

"I know," I say. "Down the road where it bends back toward town. Delilah told me. But she said that she lives alone. She didn't say your mother lived with her."

"Miss Henderson, my grandmother passed away two years ago. It was shortly after your grandfather went to the nursing home. Now my mother lives in Delilah's house."

Had I misunderstood her? I know I was exhausted from the long drive, but could I be that wrong? Bobby is in the kitchen, lighting the gas stove. Delilah said that she left a phone number in the basket, so I go to the kitchen to get it so I can show it to him.

I walk into the kitchen and Bobby turns to look at me at the very same time I look at the counter and see no baskets of food. No phone number. Nothing.

"I'm sorry," I say. "I drove all the way from New York, and I was exhausted when I got here yesterday. I'm sure I just misunderstood."

"That's probably it," Bobby says. "Well, you're all set for hot water, heat, and cooking. Now all you need are some folks to help you spruce things up a little, and you'll be good to go. Do you have kids?"

"No, it's just me," I say.

"It's a mighty big house for just one person. Will you be okay all by yourself?"

"I'll be fine," I say. "I won't be alone."

The Pencil Sketch
Carolyn Robbins

Black on white,
The pencil dances
Its errant path
Devoid of color

One moment
Hesitant and soft,
The next
Bold and sure.
But always,
Devoid of color

Yet finished,
The resulting image
Brings color
To the soul.

Invisible Music

Chris Negron

I brought three things to Hakone: the violin bow I stole from my cousin when we were children, a photograph of his dead father, and the papers I had to convince him to sign.

Upon arriving in the scenic lake town outside Mt. Fuji, I hesitated under the cover of the train station's exit, watching steady rain overflow gutters and rush down streets. It had been raining that day, too, in winter five years ago, when my father's brother and his family visited us. My cousin Kaito, though younger than me, was already much more accomplished. A math wizard and musical savant, he had brought along his violin. When I saw it in his arms, I had judged him arrogant and pretentious, a show-off, only later learning the idea to drag the instrument three hundred miles by train hadn't been his. It had been my father's.

"Following dinner," Father announced as he accepted the violin case from my cousin. "Kaito will play for us."

But my cousin never played that night. I made sure of that. And then, barely two weeks later, his parents would be dead, and Kaito would have nothing left. Not his violin, not his math trophies, not his sheet music, not even his books.

Outside the station, I popped open my umbrella and, without pausing, hurried past the waiting line of cabs parked on the street, cold rain showering their running engines, wisps of steam drifting from their hoods. Father hadn't given me money for cab rides, only enough for the train.

"Lawyers are too expensive," he had grumbled at me. "You are eighteen now. This trip is for your grandmother. You must take responsibility for her. She is your blood."

My grandfather had died a month ago. He had been caring for my frail grandmother for almost a decade. After the funeral, my father decided to take her into our home. As we drove to pick her up, he began speaking to me, answering a question I had stopped asking years before. "The situation with Kaito was different. Times were not good then, not for anyone. Certainly not for me." He paused and bit his lip, as if convincing himself the words he spoke next would be true. "It was better to let him go to the orphanage. He has been happy. Besides…"

Besides, I finished for him, Grandmother has money. And Kaito? What did he have when we were invited to take him in after the tsunami? Nothing. 3.11 stole not only his parents, but all his possessions, too. My cousin became merely another mouth to feed.

"Besides," my father continued. "The two of you never got along." He nodded and grunted, as though he'd succeeded in balancing two sides of a difficult math equation.

A week after the tsunami, Father went to see Kaito. I thought he would return with my cousin but instead he came back alone. He went straight to his desk and poured himself a whiskey, didn't respond when my mother told him dinner was ready. I remembered only the silhouette of his bowed head in that dark room, the occasional clink of ice against the side of his glass.

Rounding the corner in Hakone, I began the halting descent past a ramen shop and down the next hill. The orphanage, four floors of graying façade, loomed across the street. I stared at it, searching for dark figures lurking behind loose white curtains. I wondered if I would even recognize Kaito if I found him gazing back at me. I adjusted my grip on the bag, the bow and papers shifting inside, and almost turned back toward the station before picturing my father's disapproving glower should I come home empty-handed.

The young girl at the front desk, her long black hair swaying across her back as she spun to greet me, ran her finger down a sheet until she found Kaito's name. She asked me to sign in, then made a quick phone call.

I glanced around. Children were everywhere, clustered in corners, stacked on stairs, in circles on the floor. Five years after the magnitude 9 Tōhoku quake struck, these orphanages were still overcrowded.

"Director Yoshida will collect you soon." The girl held my gaze a long moment. I felt exposed, undressed, as if she could see my lies and crimes and insecurities written across my face. Looking down, I mumbled a thank you, then turned away.

Alone in the waiting room, I unzipped my bag, peeking at the contents. I pulled at the bow inside, rubbing my fingers along its fraying hair. At least once per week I had removed it from the concealed compartment in the back of my closet to inspect it. To my eyes, it deteriorated with each passing day. I witnessed, perhaps imagined, the smallest of changes. Hairs loosened, the polish on the wood faded, tiny nicks appeared at each end. I felt helpless to stop these slow workings of time, a desperate need to find a way to care for it. But I was afraid if I took it to a music shop, even just to buy a cake of rosin, someone would discover what I had done. My theft from my cousin had become a lie that could not be untold.

Five years had passed since I'd last seen Kaito, since the night I was so unwilling to allow someone else to impress my father. For me, all of high school, living in the same house, the same room. For Kaito, a constant shuffle from one orphanage to another, never in one place for more than a handful of months. Minamisanriku to Sendai to Kamakura to…I had lost track.

Every few months, a thick envelope would arrive by mail, addressed to my father. He would retreat to his desk, open it, and examine the documents inside. Once I asked him about them. "This is news of your cousin," he told me.

"How is he doing?"

Father had tucked the papers back into the envelope and looked away from me, out his window. "It does not say. It only tells me where he is." I waited for more information, but none came. "Go play one of your games," he said without turning to face me.

The night I stole the bow would not leave my memory. My mother had made mackerel cooked in miso, spending careful minutes preparing the fish, slicing the ginger. During the meal, my father admired Kaito's delicate hands, pointing out how clean the nails adorning the tops of my cousin's slender fingers were. He never glanced in my direction.

Later, after I had excused myself, snuck into the front room, and stolen Kaito's bow, we gathered in the formal room. The five of us knelt in a circle while Kaito went to retrieve his violin. He paused as he opened the case, gazing at the latch. A long moment passed before he looked up at our fathers and spoke. "I am sorry. I must have forgotten my bow."

My father and uncle took turns examining his case. "This is very unlike you," my uncle said to his son. He turned to my father, his eyes narrow. "It is unlike Kaito to forget," he repeated. The two brothers locked eyes and my father inhaled before lowering his head. The unspoken words they exchanged hung in the air like a black cloud.

Father turned to me, his mouth a flat, grim line. "What do you know of this?" he asked.

My lie came without hesitation. "Nothing."

I wanted to say more, to assure him the bow wasn't here, that it must be somewhere else, very far away. I wanted my father to believe finding the bow was impossible. But fear these lies would expose my act kept them locked away inside me.

My uncle and his family left early and with few words. From my window, I watched as Kaito hung his head in the back of their taxi. Did he believe he could have forgotten his bow? Did he suspect I had taken it?

For more than a week, if I made the mistake of looking into my father's eyes, I found them gazing straight back into mine, a knowing scowl in his expression. Kaito had not found his bow at home. My father questioned me daily and I feared he would soon discover the truth. But then the earthquake and tsunami came, my father's brother and his wife were killed, and he never again spoke of the night of their final visit.

As the years passed, I forgot about my cousin at times, in the way you forget about relatives you don't see. I viewed the bow less and less. Once per week became once per month. The time I spent sitting quietly in my room waiting for the opportunity to inspect the bow again was replaced by afternoons in shopping centers with friends, evenings hanging out under the bright electric lights of Akihabara.

One night, while my parents attended one of my father's important company dinners, I stayed home watching television. A documentary called "Remembering 3.11" aired. It mesmerized me. The filmmaker had spent time in the most devastated areas, interviewing those left behind: Ishinomaki, Rikuzentakata, Kamaishi, Miyako. Minamisanriku. In each city, video had been captured of the devastating water crashing over seawalls, pushing huge ships up streets into buildings, slamming cars against one another. The victims talked of and cried over the family members they lost, the treasured objects big and small that disappeared with them. Family photographs and wedding pictures. Ancient swords. Kimonos.

That night, I retrieved the bow from its hiding place and examined it. It gleamed back at me, the moonlight streaming in from my window glinting off the polished edge of the wood. For the briefest of moments, I thought perhaps I felt what my cousin must have when he looked upon it, that wide-eyed wonder I had so envied.

Rapid footsteps came up the stairs. My parents were home early. In a rush, I wedged the bow back into its hiding place, but it caught on something. The footsteps reached the top of the landing. I shoved the bow hard and, as it slid along what it had been stuck on, some jagged edge, I heard the grating sound of screeching wood. An hour later, in the dark quiet of my room, my parents fast asleep, I checked the bow again, only to find a fresh scratch, deep and wide, marring the full length of one side. I began looking at the bow more frequently again. Once per month became once per week.

Many nights I didn't sleep well. My dreams were filled with underwater concerts, symphonies of small children. They motioned the playing of their instruments, violins and cellos, with empty hands, holding no bows, making their invisible music for hours on end.

A glug of water returned me to the orphanage's waiting room. The young receptionist was refilling her glass from the dispenser in the nearby hallway. I looked up to find her staring at my hands and hurried to push the bow back deep into my bag.

As I repositioned it, the bow brushed against the papers, sliding across them, hungry to create sound again but instead causing only an ordinary ruffling of the pages of my grandfather's revised will. The original had declared that a generous inheritance would be split between his two sons, my father and uncle, to be used for the sole purpose of caring for their mother until her death. It hadn't been changed in years. Following his death, my uncle's half had been placed into a trust, to mature and be given to Kaito on his eighteenth birthday.

"Lawyers," my father muttered. "That money is meant for your grandmother. Yet half cannott be touched. Who knows how long she will live? It can't help Kaito. Not anymore." He had spoken these words to me while standing in our kitchen. Behind him, my grandmother listed to one side in her wheelchair, half asleep. I didn't think she would live to see the year change again. "No. We will surely need the other half," my father declared.

And so, though "lawyers are too expensive," he had visited one and the will had been revised to state he would have access to Kaito's share "only in the event Mrs. Nakano should need it for her continued well-being." Grandmother signed it with a trembling hand, my father helping her scrawl her name across the page. It needed only Kaito's signature to be official.

At first I refused Father's command to visit my cousin with the papers, terrified of doing what I knew I would have to if I made the journey to Hakone–return the bow, confess my crime. If he wanted his papers signed, Father would have to go himself.

"I have to work, Jiro. This should be done quickly, for your grandmother's sake." Then, before I could protest further, he opened a desk drawer and extracted a small photograph, handing it to me. It was a black-and-white picture of my father and uncle as young men, around my age, dressed in suits and posing in front of Mt. Fuji. They appeared confident, ready to take on the world. "Take that to your cousin as well. It cannot hurt."

When I looked up from the picture and began to question him about when the photo had been taken and why, by whom, he interrupted me. "Show no one but Kaito those papers."

The discussion was over. I steeled my nerves. I had waited years to return the bow. Now I also had a picture of my uncle to give to my cousin. After the destruction of their family's home, this might be the only image of his father Kaito would ever see again. Perhaps returning these small things could somehow lessen my crime against him. So I packed the papers into my bag with the bow and photograph and walked to Shinjuku station to visit my cousin.

"Mr. Nakano?" The tall man asking for me stood in the doorway to the waiting room, holding a clipboard. "This way, please."

I followed Director Yoshida up a flight of stairs into his crowded office. Mountains of file folders and paper created a labyrinth-like entry. The director fell into his chair with an exhalation. I sat across from him as he pulled a file from the top of the nearest stack. "So. Kaito Nakano. And you are—" He checked the clipboard again. "His cousin?"

"Yes. Jiro."

"Jiro." He tested the name as he perused the contents of Kaito's file. "Jiro. We always appreciate family visits, Jiro, but I must ask…" He stopped and pushed his glasses up on his nose. "Kaito hasn't received a visitor in a very long time now."

He hadn't asked a question, but I felt the pressure of his curiosity nonetheless. With a few words he had judged my entire family. "I—" The revised will pressed hot against my leg, through the bag on the floor at my side. "Our grandfather died."

Director Yoshida leaned back in his chair again, raising his steepled fingers to his chin. "Yes, well, I was afraid it might be bad news." He glanced down, seemed to consider what he should say next. "I'm sorry for your loss. But you must understand that Kaito is far from the boy you may have known. I cannot prevent you from telling him anything you might wish to, but you should consider…" He hesitated. I waited. "I assume you've seen the reports regarding his fear of the coast?"

"No." I thought of the thick envelopes my father received, the ones he opened in private. I wondered what had really been in them and felt warmth spread up from my neck into my face.

"Kaito has been transferred many times." Sendai, Kamakura, Hakone. "It took a number of coastal locations to determine it would be best for him to be somewhere with a higher elevation." The director pointed out his window, at his view of Lake Ashi. Beyond the lake, in the distance with its snow-covered cap, loomed Fuji. "The mountain comforts him."

"And the lake?" I asked. "If he is afraid of water, then why is he here?"

Director Yoshida spread his hands. "Small steps. His doctors feel a view of the lake may help him conquer his fears of the water. Sometimes he seems to enjoy it. But most days your cousin is focused on what he lost. He spends a great deal of time searching for his possessions on the Internet. And that isn't healthy. He has the highest room in the building, one of the best views of the mountain. And a computer. Not all of the children are so lucky." He opened the file again. "The money from your grandfather has ensured we can provide these…privileges. You say he's passed on?"

I reached down and clutched at my bag, felt the shape of the bow and, behind it, the papers. "Yes, but there is a trust."

"Of course," he said, inclining his head.

I stood and pulled the bag up with me. "May I see him now?"

We climbed two more flights of stairs, traveling further along austere white corridors, right and left, left and right, until we reached Kaito's room. "I would ask that you avoid the subjects of the tsunami or his parents, the things he's lost," the director said before knocking on my cousin's door. Together we waited in uncomfortable silence.

Kaito had been nine when I saw him last, tiny, almost frail. I remembered wondering, with some disdain, how everyone could claim his miniscule hands were able to play the violin so adeptly. The boy who opened the door, however, was fourteen, already taller than me, his moppy hair dangling in front of his eyes and the posture of his rail thin form stooped and uncertain. His hands were no longer enviably delicate, his fingers anything but slender.

"Hello, Kaito," Director Yoshida said. My cousin didn't respond. His dark eyes focused on me for a moment before growing distant again. "Look. Your cousin Jiro has come to visit."

Kaito and I stared at each other a long moment, me in the hallway, him in his room, as if the line dividing the two spaces was dangerous to cross, a canyon. I thought I should say something, but I wasn't sure what. "I'm sorry I haven't come sooner," I told him.

"They found a violin bow in Oregon," he said brightly before lowering his voice. "It wasn't mine." I felt my breath catch and peeked to see if the director noticed my reaction but he only watched Kaito as he shuffled backwards, leaving the door open, a sort of invitation for me to enter.

"One of the things he lost when he was young," Director Yoshida whispered in my ear. "It seems to bother your cousin most, as if he could've done something to save the bow. He's requested a violin but we don't allow instruments here. The noise. You understand." I didn't but said nothing. "The doctors do bring him bows they find in markets or donation centers." He gestured to Kaito, who had pulled a box from under his bed, lifted it to his desk, and removed the lid. It was full of bows in varied states of disrepair, some with hair and some without, some scratched and nicked, mangled even, others almost ready for use.

"Good luck," the director said as he began to move away. Inside the room, Kaito worked to set each bow out in careful order on his desk, lining them up parallel to one another.

I stepped over the threshold, hesitant, as if I were doing more than entering a room. I felt like I might be walking into the past. When I came within a few feet of Kaito, his gaze darted toward me, as though he was surprised to discover my presence. Then, his eyes distant as if he'd forgotten me just as quickly, he paced over to his computer. I followed, watching over his shoulder as he shook the mouse to wake the machine. He began moving from one open tab to another in his browser, refreshing each page as he passed through them.

His hand moved too quickly for me to follow. But when he landed on the final tab, he paused long enough for me to notice it was a Facebook page full of photographs. He lifted his gaze to his window, the same view of the lake and mountain as in the director's office, but here from a higher vantage point. After a few moments he returned his focus to the computer and scrolled down to the photograph of a violin bow covered in barnacles and seaweed, a woman's delicate hand angling it for the camera.

Kaito tapped the monitor screen with his finger, shaking his head. "It wasn't mine." Then he returned to the job of extracting the bows from his box and lining them up a few feet away.

Eyeing him, I took control of the mouse and inspected the page. An environmental group in the American state of Oregon had set up a tsunami debris program. They were using Facebook to publicize their findings and return them to their Japanese owners. Most of the photographs featured a smiling Japanese woman. She often stood next to a tall, sandy-haired American man. The photograph of the violin bow was three years old. I scrolled all the way to the top of the page, past skiffs and medals, slippers, sneakers and jewelry, soccer balls. The most recent post was nearly two years old. The group had either stopped finding things or stopped trying.

Kaito remained focused on the bows. I took the opportunity to inspect the other open tabs. There were at least a dozen of them, all similar pages displaying debris recovery programs, some on Facebook like the Oregon one, others blogs and websites. The programs were in Washington and California, Canada and Alaska. One was a museum in British Columbia, another a lone old man, a career beachcomber. None had been updated in the past year, yet my cousin had refreshed them as though he expected breaking news at any moment.

I didn't think he was paying attention to me, head down, precise fingers aligning the tips of each bow, but after I read the last page and stood straight up, Kaito peered over at me. "I check all the pages. Every day. Many people are finding many things."

Kaito stepped back and exhaled. His eyes widened, as if seeing me clearly for the first time. "You were there. The night I lost my bow. Do you remember?"

"I do," I said. The bag had become too heavy to hold. I set it on the ground.

"Father and I looked and looked at home," Kaito said. "We couldn't find it. He was going to buy me a new one that weekend. The tsunami came on a Friday." He headed toward his door and I thought he might leave but instead he closed it. He lingered there, back turned, and I saw that excited nine-year-old, ready to buy a brand new bow with his father. I slid his bow from my bag. Kaito continued, his voice low. "They took us to the school's roof."

I aligned my bow—his bow—with the others, parallel as Kaito had done. I pulled my hand away. He turned. Our eyes met.

"We could see them running," he said, hushed. "The people. 'Run!' my teacher yelled to them as they rushed toward us." He took a few steps back into the room, reared up and yelled. "Run!" I cringed.

My cousin paced toward the desk again. He inspected the bows, his hand hovering over each one, grazing them, until he stopped on the new addition. I held my breath.

"Run," Kaito whispered. He sniffed. "They weren't fast enough."

"I'm sorry." It was all I could say, because sorrow was all I felt. I was sorry I stole his bow, that his parents had died. I was sorry we hadn't visited him. I was sorry he was alone. "Kaito, are you happy here?"

My cousin gazed out the window again, looking at Fuji. His hand didn't move away from his bow. "It came so fast. We were on the roof, did I tell you that?"

"Yes, you did," I whispered.

He smiled for the first time. "Here, I have both the mountain and the lake. You see? I am always happy." He looked down again, at my bow. Or, the one I had brought with me. His. He picked it up and held it to the light of the lamp on his desk, ran his finger along the deep scratch. The slow movement of that finger raised goose bumps on my arms. "I used to play for them at night," he said. "My parents. I still do, sometimes."

He hefted an invisible violin to his chin and, with the bow he hadn't touched in five years, he began to play. His eyes were closed. He swayed to the music he produced, though there was none there. In the dream I still remembered from years ago, the symphony of underwater children held instruments they attempted to play with invisible bows. Now Kaito stood in front of me, playing an invisible violin with his own, real bow.

I should have told him about our grandfather. I should have warned him about my father. I should have let him know the bow he held was really his. Maybe he already knew. But I did none of these things. Instead I let him play. I would never stop him from playing again.

I didn't move until he finished and bowed. Then, I applauded.

Kaito laid the bow back amongst the rest. I glanced at my bag, resting on the floor, the papers still inside, and I knew they wouldn't come out. I realized I had known this when I put them in. Then I remembered the photograph. "I have something for you."

I slipped the picture from the pocket inside my bag and gave it to him. He turned it over and stared at it, his eyes intent, lips parting slightly. I didn't need to wonder if he recognized his father. He paced over to his window and held it up, matching his view of the mountain with the image in the picture.

I had a sudden idea. "Kaito. How about we take a picture?" I held up my phone.

"Of me?"

I smiled and clicked out the little stand that had come with my new mobile. "Of us."

Crossing the room, I propped the phone up on his nightstand, checking the position. Satisfied, I set the timer and hurried back. "Stand up straight and smile," I said, then started to countdown from ten. Halfway, I nudged him. "Straight, Kaito." My cousin released a short burst of laughter and we finished the count together. "Three, two, one…" The flash went off.

We checked the result together. In our picture, my cousin and I stood next to each other in sweatshirts and jeans, a sharp contrast to the suits our fathers had worn in theirs. But Mt. Fuji rose up behind us in just the same way. We stood straight, side by side. We smiled. Our poses were the same. Nothing else was.

I checked the clock on Kaito's wall. My return ticket left in an hour and I still had to walk back to the station in the continuing rain. There was nothing left to do here. I had given my cousin his bow and the photograph. I could give him nothing more.

"I'll send you a copy," I said, raising my phone. "But I have to go now. I'm sorry."

My cousin lowered his head but said nothing.

"I'll come back," I told him. "Promise."

Kaito looked up and smiled. I remembered it, that smile, from when he was young, before the earth had trembled, forcing the ocean to raise its fist and crash down on his life, stealing it away.

I turned back one last time from the hallway. He had returned to his computer, re-opening his browser and scrolling through the tabs, refreshing them one by one, again and again. I stood there watching him. When he turned, a flash of recognition sparked in his eyes. "You were there. The night I lost my bow. Do you remember?"

I felt a weight press down on my shoulders and settle into my chest. "I remember, Kaito."

He nodded, stood and gathered up the bows on his desk, paying no more attention to the one that had been his than any of the others. I eased his door closed.

That night when my father arrived home from work, he came straight to my room. He asked, hands extended as though I had the signed papers waiting to drop into them, whether I had found Kaito.

"No," I told him.

"What do you mean?" my father asked. "Where is he?"

I stared into his wild eyes. "He's somewhere very far away," I said, refusing to blink. "It's not possible to find him anymore."

This time, I wasn't lying.

Playing Along
Megan Benoit Ratcliff

"What the hell is wrong with me?"
I think,
Catching myself
Eyes closed in bed
With pursed lips and furrowed brow.
No wonder
Wrinkles are appearing,
"C" creases on my
Prematurely
(but maybe not really at age 37)
Age spotted cheeks.

Pursed lips by night,
Fake smile by day,
Plastered on,
While I nod and listen
To the bullshit
That is
What other people want
Other people to believe
About their
secretly
discontented lives.

What is wrong with me
Is that I am playing along.

Sparrow

Mary Wivell

Marriage is like bird watching. When it's fresh and new, every species of sparrow constitutes a thrill. Even the sight of a black-headed cardinal, bald from post-nuptial molting, delights. Time goes on, bliss fades and you're left with fewer and fewer surprises.

We were guilty. After the birth of our second son, date nights had devolved into errand evenings, with trips to Home Depot, all lists and panic. We're practical people. Save money, vacation seldom, family bed, but these practices were wearing a little thin.

A friend of a friend had a place on the Gulf Coast and asked did we want to join them? Yes. Desperate to escape the Northern winter, I sold my husband on the idea. "The children'll have their own room. We'll be alone," I said. Untrue. I knew quarters would be cramped. The boys would sleep in our room, but that didn't matter. Our bed hadn't seen much action since our second child arrived. And this was despite my hubby's expressed desire to have another baby, one of our many unresolved arguments that percolated resentment. A change of scene might help, right? Maybe we'll go birding, I told him, though I doubted it.

We'd worked out a deal. Each couple would get one night out. The others parents would watch the kids. It wasn't a fair deal. The other family had three children. Three. Why on earth would anyone have that many kids? But they were happy. At the airport, they'd rented a convertible. Us? We selected a minivan.

###

"Damn it," I said, "we're going on a date."

"Aw, I don't know," he trailed off, fitting a valve into the lid of a sippy cup.

"Tonight's our night." I folded a beach towel from the basket, wondering if I'd need to do another load.

"The thing is..." he started. But I knew what he was going to say, knew he'd suggest we 'hang out' and drink beer by the pool near the bug zapper.

"No." I tried to keep my voice nice, worked hard to smile while I said, "We're on the flippin' Flamabama coast and we're—"

He interrupted, "Emerald Coast—" He's from Florida. "You know, people travel from all over the world to visit beaches here—" Now it was my turn to interrupt.

"Florida. Alabama. Redneck Riviera," I sang out. "Whatever—Listen, we get one night without the kids and we're going to do something that we can only do *here*."

"Like what?"

"Field trip." I smiled and rounded the counter to take his hand. "Let's go looking for the red cockaded wood-pecker."

"Bird watching?"

"Yeah."

"Can't do it. Prescribed burns this week. Remember the signs?"

I did. 'Danger Smoke Area' and 'Prescribed Burn' signs had dotted the road. Forest rangers were setting the pines on fire.

"Planned burns," I said, slipping around behind him and reaching up, my hands massaging his shoulders. "Sounds like scheduling sex. Can't they just let it happen naturally?"

"Right," he said, his shoulders loosening as I kneaded. "Like lightning?"

"No, more like, invite bored locals to drink beer and whoop it up until Billy Bob and Becky Sue get careless with their cigarette butts."

He turned his face toward me and grinned. "They burn it one stretch at a time, so maybe..."

"We'll borrow the convertible, find an unburned spot. It'll be fun, promise."

Ask my husband if he's a birdwatcher and he'll deny it.

"Call him a 'birdwatcher's companion,'" I'd advised our friends. He didn't think it was funny.

Before kids, he accompanied me on birding trips, followed me along beaches stalking Wilson's phalarope, hiked mountains in search of pygmy nuthatches, waited for hours alongside rivers, silent and listening, until we sighted the yellow breasted chat.

As newlyweds, we'd beheld some magical finds. Honeymooning on Kauai, we trekked steep jungle paths, made treacherous by driving rain, netting several species of honeycreepers. A Western tanager alit on a branch above our heads when we'd paused our mountain bikes in a Colorado state park. Bullock's oriole, blue-gray gnatcatcher, same park. Summer tanagers greeted us in a parking lot near a South Carolina coastal swamp. Nesting eagles, plunging osprey, sandhill cranes by the side of the road, Eastern blue birds—they came to us.

More recently, both bird outings and marital bliss had become rarer than the California condor.

A few hours later, after a long conversation about the convertible and the nuances of auto insurance, we were driving our rented mini-van along Route 414, a rural two lane that passed few houses. Blacktop wavered in the heat. Pine trees and palmettos stretched as far as the eye could see. He drove. I sipped Chardonnay from a plastic cup.

"Listen to this," I said, paraphrasing from a regional field guide, "'The endangered *Picoides borealis,* otherwise known as the red-cockaded woodpecker, has painted itself into an ecological corner. Red cocks nest only in long leaf pines over 40 years old.'"

I silently skimmed the rest of the article.

"Not only do the trees have to be old, but they have to have been burned in a fire, and then recovered, and then infested with some particular species of rot." And he calls me high-maintenance.

"Okay," he said, sounding bored, "but where will we park?"

How the hell should I know? I thought. Instead, I patted his knee gently and said, "We'll figure it out, honey."

Finding the birds wouldn't be easy. It was breeding season, and we hoped that would figure in our favor. We'd park near nest sites just before dusk and wait for the fickle birds to return from foraging.

Sure enough, an hour inland we spotted the trees, marked by wildlife managers, just as the article described, their trunk bases coated in white paint.

"Pull over," I shouted.

"Where?" asked my husband, mildly irritated.

"Anywhere."

"Not safe."

On we drove.

More nest sites, more trees. Dusk was approaching; we needed to find a place soon.

Finally we spotted a little turn-off with a ring of nest sites in the rear. He pulled the mini-van along the rutted red dirt lane. Mosquitoes smashed themselves against the windows like bloodthirsty kamikazes. Through the bug-splattered windshield, we spotted egg-shaped holes in the trees, a telltale sign of the woodpeckers' roosts. The sun perched on the horizon. The birds might arrive any minute.

"Hurry." I climbed out, uncapping my binoculars.

He followed at a leisurely pace.

Five minutes passed—five full minutes of my husband slapping his arms and legs. We stood, side-by-side watching the black empty holes.

"These bugs," slap, slap, "are eating me alive." He jingled the keys. "I'll wait in the car."

This had happened once before. On an anniversary trip, sans children, to Michigan's Upper Peninsula, the bugs were devouring him. He hiked back to the car and left me alone to explore Estivant Pines. An inaccurate map and a careless turn led me astray. Lost, I circled back. For an hour, I retraced my steps, listening to approaching thunder from a storm rolling in off Superior. It was terrifying.

Now, alone, I wandered down the rutted road, the sky honey-soaked. The pines smelled fresh, my steps cushioned by a blanket of brown needles. But I couldn't enjoy myself with him sitting in the car. We'd both doused ourselves with Off!, but by this time the mosquitoes were circling me, buzzing in my ears. In hopes of eluding them, I kept moving, watching all the while, listening.

Cheery calls from Carolina chickadees mocked my desperation.

Movement in a pine revealed only a lone chipping sparrow, rusty headed, common as the red Panhandle dirt under my feet.

We were leaving in two days. Would we ever get another chance to see the red cocks? Now was the time.

The sight of the nest holes, so stark earlier, faded into the dark trunks in the diminishing light. I felt a tickle on my neck, slapped. My hand came away bloodied. A tickle on my leg meant they were biting through my pants. Desperate, I wanted to wait, but instead retreated to the car.

I ran and clamored inside as quickly as I could.

"Did you see anything?"

"Not unless you count a chipping sparrow."

We listened to the night, cicadas and crickets. Minutes passed to full dark. A loaded log truck barreled down the highway.

"Want to leave?"

"Let's wait."

We sat in silence. We didn't talk about our jobs, or the balloon mortgage hanging over our heads. We didn't gripe about the state of government, or the in-laws, or the fact that he wanted another child and I didn't.

How it started, I cannot say, but there's something I call 'Hot Married Sex.' You can fill in the blanks with your own dirty mind. I hadn't been party to back seat sex since high school, but I can tell you that a minivan is a very practical choice for all sorts of activities.

"Cigarette?" he asked, afterward, tipping an imaginary pack my way.

"I'll do you one better," I said as I reached for my bag and drew out a stale pack of Winstons, one of my few secrets in more than a decade of unbridled marital honesty.

He took it pretty well.

Maybe he already knew.

"Hey, we should've smoked these out there." He nodded to the pines. "Might've kept the mosquitoes away."

Smoke coiled around my head. I waved it away and asked if he'd ever seen the bumper sticker that read, *'If this van is rockin', don't' come a' knockin''*.

"Ha, how 'bout the one that says, '*I scream truck*'?"

We laughed.

A few minute passed. Smoke filled the van. I wondered if the rental car company would charge us extra, but squelched the desire to voice my concern.

"Ready?" he asked.

"Ready."

We cracked a window and drove back. The fires alongside the highway burned steady. Yellow and orange flames ate back undergrowth, hopefully readying the pines for future generations of red-cockaded woodpeckers.

###

Nine months later, I gave birth to a little girl. We named her Kiran.

But we call her Sparrow.

Angels to the Rescue

Terry Segal

I've always heard the voices of angels. I'm neither psychotic nor a religious fanatic. As a child, I didn't know whose voices they were. I just knew they were comforting and different from anything else I had ever heard. I didn't have running conversations with them, but I'd be aware of a gentle voice, accompanied by a deeply peaceful presence I felt whenever I needed it.

One time, when I was about six or seven years old, a dog trapped me in our next-door neighbor's backyard. The mom there knew I was terrified of him. She was kind, though, and whenever I went over to play with their visiting cousin, she always put the dog outside. On that day, however, her son, mean-spirited Duncan, almost three years older than I, told me that his cousin was out back and that the dog was at the vet with his mom. I went through the house and outside to the yard. I didn't see my friend and ventured farther out, calling her name. Suddenly, Duncan opened the door with a sinister look on his face, as Studebaker, the nightmare dog, ran past him and charged toward me. Duncan closed the door from the inside.

I shrieked and ran in circles as the dog nipped at my legs and hands. As a ballerina who was definitely not a fence climber, I decided the fence was my only chance to escape. I squeezed my right foot, sideways, into the chain link, then my left foot in the next one above that, and tried to scramble up and over the top. Duncan opened the door, doubled over, holding his stomach and laughing, before going back inside again.

Pain shot through the underside of my thigh. I pictured Studebaker's sharp teeth piercing my skin but it was the barbed wire they had put on their fence to keep him from leaping over into other yards. The dog, with his fat, stubby legs and lion's teeth, kept bounding off the ground to get to me. I had thrown the back of my leg over the fence and didn't care if I might face-plant on the hard earth, as long as I landed in my own yard. I just wanted to get away from Studebaker.

But that didn't happen. I was caught at the top of the fence, blood dripping down my leg, and collecting at the cuff of my crisp, new, white sock. The wire was all snagged in the hole it had ripped in my favorite peach Sherbet-colored shorts. I straddled the fence in pain, crying, still horrified at the persistence of this dog who was trying to eat me alive.

Suddenly, I felt a sensation of arms around me. Not arms exactly (and now I know that they were wings), but I experienced being held, solidly and gently. My knotted stomach muscles relaxed and I could breathe again. Studebaker was still jumping and yapping but it was somehow muted.

I took a deep breath from the bottom of my belly and yelled, "Help me! Please help me!" I was hoping that Duncan might have a change of heart or that my mom could hear me, but she had been vacuuming the house when I left.

I heard a voice call out, "I'm coming! Where are you?"

I repeated, "I'm over here. Here!"

A twelve-year-old boy named Jose, from a few blocks away, had been walking to get an Icee at the 7-Eleven store. We called back and forth until he saw me and rushed to unlatch the gate to my yard. He stood close to the fence and extended his arms upward. He told me to reach down to his shoulders and that he would lift me and bring me down safely. As he did, I felt as if I floated until my feet gently touched the ground. I sobbed with relief and gratitude.

From that day on, I knew there were forces greater than ourselves who are here to help us. I realized that we have to help ourselves, too. I told my parents what had happened and that night they called Duncan's mother. I never went back to Duncan's house again, but when his cousin came to my house to play, she told me he had gotten in big trouble. Angels, forgive me, but I have to admit I was more than a little bit glad.

HUMOR-1

Christmas in Jacktown — **Tom Leidy**

Enjoy! — **John Sheffield**

Days of Destiny — **Tom Leidy**

Two Countries Divided by Geography — **John Sheffield**

Christmas in Jacktown

Tom Leidy

During the Great Depression my father worked as a lay preacher in a Methodist church and as "boysinger" in the swing bands so popular then.

The bands played engagements in supper clubs and dance halls, hotels and resorts, high schools and colleges in Ohio, West Virginia, Michigan, and Pennsylvania. Dad also played trumpet. His horn and mute and wah-wah hat are gone, but we've saved many newspaper ads and promotional items for the bands he played with and a few of his recordings. Over the years, Dad told us many stories about his experiences with the bands. Most times, though, we didn't really listen. As he got older and began repeating himself, we would tell the most docile grandchild to, "Go listen to Granddad."

Soon after Mom and Dad were married in West Virginia in 1932, they moved into a little one-bedroom house in Jacksontown ("Jacktown") Ohio, where U.S. 40 (The National Road) crosses Ohio Route 13 south of Newark. The house is there still, beside a white frame Methodist church, on a small hill just outside Jacktown.

They lived rent free. For that, Mom and Dad maintained the church and the area around it and Dad preached Sunday mornings, but not always in Jacktown. Many small communities then could not afford full time ministers for all their churches. So, working together, they created a kind of circuit: ministers and lay preachers in towns up and down Route 40 traveling Sundays to one church or another. Mom and Dad rotated through Methodist churches in Jacktown, Somerset, Hebron, Gratiot ("Gray Shot"), and Buckeye Lake. Baptists and Presbyterians and Congregationalists did the same and every Sunday each community on the circuit had a service somewhere.

The summer of 1933 my mother's apparent pregnancy caused a minor furor.

During the Depression birth rates were significantly reduced, producing a dip or "ditch" in the historically steady pace of population growth. I was one of those "ditch" babies and any birth in the area at that time was an exciting event. Soon, Mom and Dad were returning from their journeys up and down Route 40 with hand-made, "hardly-ever-been-used" booties and sweaters, nappies, and other baby requirements.

As summer faded to fall the range and types of gifts grew to include food and canned goods and, sometimes, money. Not much. Usually only a dollar or two. I have a little notebook Dad kept from 1930 through 1940. It shows, by date and location, the money he earned. One or two dollars doesn't seem like much now, but when bread cost five cents a loaf and gasoline ten cents a gallon, a dollar went a long way.

To show gratitude for all their kindnesses, Mom and Dad wanted to do something for Christmas for their friends and families on the circuit, something that could be shared in all Dad's churches. They decided the ideal gift would be a set of hymnals they could carry from church to church. Dad wrote the Methodist Publishing House in Cincinnati requesting a price list.

When the list arrived though, all the books were far more expensive than they could afford. But hymnals was such a good idea Mom and Dad were reluctant to give it up. Perhaps, they thought, they could work out some sort of payment plan or other arrangement. Dad called long distance to Cincinnati, a major expense then.

"No," he was told. "Times being what they are, we don't give credit."

"Don't you have anything we could afford, used books, maybe, or damaged books?"

"No, we have nothing like that. We do have one set of books that might fit your budget, but people don't really like using them."

"Why not?"

"They have advertising all through them."

"Well, thank you. We'll think about it."

So, Mom and Dad thought about it. What kind of advertising could there be in a hymn book? Choir Robes? Altar Cloths? Collection Plates? Pew Cushions? Just after Thanksgiving, Dad called Cincinnati again.

"Do you still have those hymn books with the advertising in them?"

"Yes sir."

"Okay. We'll send you a money order for one hundred books."

Through this time, Mom and Dad continued their Sunday morning rounds and Dad continued working with swing bands in the area. He made pretty good money with the bands: five to ten dollars a night.

December 21, 1933, the shortest day of the year, dawned gloomy and cold. Snow blew in the air, covered the ground, and drifted in the valleys and low areas around Newark and Jacktown. That afternoon, Mom and Dad drove their Ford coupe into Newark. Mom would spend the night at her parents' home on Elmwood Avenue. Her older sisters, Essie and Julia, lived there as well. The house is there still.

Dad borrowed Essie's Model A sedan, picked up several members of the band, and they all drove north about thirty miles up Route 13 to Mount Vernon, Ohio to play an engagement at Abe's Cave, a roadhouse just outside town. The temperature continued to drop that night to record lows and Aunt Essie's car engine froze up in the parking lot.

Many buckets of hot water over a couple of hours finally thawed it out.

Dad got back down to Elmwood Avenue about 7:00 A.M. December 22. I arrived, in the back bedroom of my grandparents' house, before he did.

But, though I had arrived, the books had not. Dad made another long distance call to Cincinnati and was assured they would be delivered by Christmas Eve.

Early December 24, Mom and Dad and I drove through light snow back down to Jacktown. The books weren't there. Dad worked that day preparing the church for a Christmas Eve service at 8:00 P.M. That afternoon the wind rose, the temperature fell, and snow blew heavier. Dad fired up the little wood-burning stove in the vestibule of the church, lit candles in the windows, and shoveled snow off the entryway. A farmer who lived close by drove his tractor over to snow plow the driveway and parking area. Still, the books had not arrived.

7:00 P.M. No books. At 7:30 Dad helped Mom and me over to the church and tucked us into a corner in the first pew down front. Then, through the windows, he saw headlights arcing up the driveway and heard the Railway Express truck grind to a stop outside the door. The books had arrived.

Dad stacked the cases behind the lectern, opened one, and took out a book. It was bound in dark blue, pebble-grained leather. *Methodist Hymnal* was stamped gold on the cover. The pages were edged gold. It had a violet silken page marker. Dad flipped through it. No choir robes. No altar cloths. No ads. The wrong set of books.

"Oh well," he thought. "It's too late now. We'll use them tonight. Maybe I'll explain everything to everyone after Christmas."

By then, people were coming in for the service. They all walked down front to see Mom and me and most of them left gifts: more nappies, diapers, knitted and crocheted things; pies and fried chicken; canned goods. Their overworked, hard bitten, wind-blown faces softened and their eyes glistened as, looking down at me and Mom, they relived for a moment sweeter times, when their lives were a joyful promise, their children tiny flowers.

The church filled. Men, some in suits and overcoats, most in winter work clothes, lined the walls. Wives and mothers and grandmothers filled the pews. Children knelt on the floor down front. Seven members of the double quartet choir sat behind the lectern. Dad, the eighth, sang tenor.Miss Englehardt was ready at the upright piano.

Burbling heat from the little stove, dusky candlelight, soft murmuring voices, shuffling feet, the mother and child, the gifts, and the unmistakable odors of wet wool and not-too-clean bodies all combined to recreate, that cold winter night in central Ohio in 1933, a scene first witnessed two thousand years ago.

Dad stepped to the lectern, thanked everyone for all their kindnesses, told them he and Mom had a gift to share as well, wished them all a blessed Christmas, and asked the double quartet to pass out the new hymnals. As the books were distributed, he and Miss Englehardt chose the first hymn. Dad announced it: *Hark, the Herald Angels Sing*.

Miss Englehardt played the introduction . . . dum dee dee dum . . . dee dum dee dum . . . and the congregation sang:

> *Hark, the herald angels sing,*
> *For Blakley's Pills—they're just the thing.*
> *Peace on earth and mercy mild,*
> *Two for a man; one for a child.*

Dad told this story every Christmas to anyone who would listen. Some of it I think might pretty much be true.

Enjoy!

John Sheffield

enjoy (injoy) vt. 1. to have or experience with joy; get pleasure from; relish.

2. to have the use of; have as one's lot or advantage.

Webster's New Dictionary of the American Language.

In primary school, I learned that words were supposed to be used in groups. The English teacher presented the case that, in groups, words had more purpose. Nevertheless, there are words that appear singly, like icebergs in the summer Atlantic. There are even those that can justifiably stand in such isolation; commands are one example, "Sit!" to a dog and "Halt!" to a trespasser.

In contrast, some do not sit comfortably alone, like proud sentinels. These words are awkward, gawky even, in their solitude. An unwelcome novice joined their ranks some years ago: "Enjoy!" Not, "I hope you are enjoying the view," or "Please enjoy your dinner," but simply "Enjoy."

Our language has sunk from the heights reached in the nimble penmanship of that pre-American, Shakespeare. Will "A rose by any other name would smell as sweet," become merely "Smell?"

I hold New Yorkers responsible for this particularly un-enjoyable misuse of the language. I sense that, in New York, they are too busy to combine words. The populace has been reduced to pithy expressions, such as "Taxi," "Happy," and "Enjoy." I was not concerned about their habit until they exported it, a fact I realized in a Chinese restaurant in Washington. My waiter deposited bowls of Mu-Shoo pork, pancakes, and rice on the table and uttered a single word: "Enjoy!"

However, one situation I had encountered, in which the telegraphic use of language was justified, was in the Spelling Bee. On the assumption that the waiter was testing me, I replied triumphantly, "E. N. J. O. Y."

Days of Destiny

Tom Leidy

I was an unimaginative child. It didn't occur to me to wonder why, early in my grammar school years, I was classified a Red Bird while many of my friends became Blue Birds.

Only in sixth grade, when we chose courses intended to lead to some sort of career path—commercial, industrial, college prep, etc.—did I realize Blue Birds were mostly college prep, Red Birds mostly not. I (and my parents) expected I'd go to college. And, to compound the mystery, I realized later my Blue Bird friends routinely got better grades in college prep courses than I did.

That combination—a college prep Red Bird not earning good grades—turned out to be kind of a back-handed blessing. Mom and Dad were happy whenever I brought home the occasional B or A on my report card and otherwise didn't mess into my academic affairs (with the unfortunate exception of Latin irregular verbs on which my Dad drilled me, mostly to no avail, after dinner night after night till Latin II ended and I had earned my usual C minus).

But I excelled in so-called special projects. Some twenty years after the fact, in my Latin teacher's living room, Mom and Dad found my signed extra-credit pastel drawing of a Roman legionnaire trumpeter hanging framed over her fireplace. And I fared well on tests of general intelligence (like College Boards today) that led to university acceptance and placement.

And so, despite my Red Bird status and less than Blue Bird grades, I enjoyed reasonable success in college, my performance dominated by what had come to be called then the 'Gentleman C'.

When I was three or four years old my grandparents gave me a two-wheel bicycle. It was small and red and, no matter how often and how fast Dad pushed me up and down Fairfield Avenue, impossible for me to ride. (Training wheels had not been invented yet.)

It was only after I saw my Blue Bird friends out skylarking on their bikes (without their fathers) I realized I probably could do it, too.

But, all too soon, my younger brother became bike ready and I was deemed eligible for a 'big' bike. I wanted a horn-in-the tank blue Roadmaster endorsed by Bob Feller, but I got a bare bones red Elgin with a propensity for broken forks and flat rear tires. Since the Elgin was frequently not rideable and I was bigger than my brother (then) I was happy to ride the little bike and for him to walk or stay home.

Orrin Key and I were not friends. During the war our town population grew dramatically (rumored to be hillbillies coming up from West Virginia coal camps to get work). Housing was difficult to find and Orrin lived with his family in a chicken coop. As such things went then, it was not a bad place—the chickens were long gone and it wasn't small—but nevertheless, it was a chicken coop.

In fifth grade Orrin sat with me at our desk. The classroom was crowded and apparently desks were as difficult to find as houses. Aside from our jockeying for space (the first one there got to sit next to the aisle) we occasionally "sabotaged" (a war-time addition to the vernacular) unguarded school work: a feather sketched on Orrin's paper; what looked like an empty ice cream cone beside a large letter U! on mine (Screw You!). Later that year Orrin caught an ear infection, dropped out of school, and later died.

Dad had taught me about basic hand tools—hammer and nails, saw, wrench and pliers, screws and screwdriver, etc.—and, though not particularly adept, I knew how to use them (but the purpose and validity of the Phillips head screw eludes me still). In fact, during those long ago lost days, I couldn't entirely understand the concept of the word 'screw'—both a verb and a noun (yet another troubling "irregular").

Though I didn't fully understand them either, my basic sexual urges were beginning to burble (after Cub Scout den meetings we all ran three blocks through the night to stand in an open field outside a window in Mimi Farmer's house and watch her get ready for bed). And though I didn't quite know what I meant, I would shout "Screw You!" (verb? noun?) at whomever needed it whenever it was appropriate.

More important to me than the dictionary definition of screw—"to drive a metal fastener with a helical thread into wood or the like by rotating (it)"—was the operational definition as it might be applied to a human screwer.

I could barely do three pushups then and thought it unlikely I ever could support myself prone above a receptive female screwee and rotate around her for any meaningful period of time to any significant effect.

By 1945 it had become apparent the United States and its allies were winning the war. I shared the general elation and anticipation of returning peace and good times (firecrackers, bubble gum, metal toy soldiers, cap guns, etc.), but only to a point (fewer war movies, no paper or scrap drives, less general excitement).

August fifth the Enola Gay destroyed Hiroshima. August sixth President Harry S Truman called it a day of destiny: ". . . a new era in man's understanding of nature's forces . . ." as he told the world a little about how it was done.

Johnny Wolfe lived up the street from me. I didn't know him well. But, having burned down the storage barn behind Beckman's grocery store, he was thought in the neighborhood to be a bad kid.

Phyllis ('Fudgie') Flannigan had started school when I did, but had to repeat first grade. Thereafter, she stayed at least two years in every grade and dropped well behind us. But she remained a good friend, and in summer all educational differences—successes and failures—were forgotten.

Late for dinner August seventh, I was careening the quick, reliable little red bike—my Chuck's on wheels—down a short-cut alley toward home and saw Johnny and Fudgie hurrying together under the apple tree in his backyard toward his garage. I turned the bike around, rode back to the garage, leaned up to a side window and, standing on the pedals, saw inside my day of destiny: a new era in my understanding of nature's forces.

There on the floor they were doing it . . . screwing. And, having seen how it was done, I knew I could do it, too. But of course, in this particular skill, knowing how it's done is not the same as actually doing it, and my chance to do it didn't come till years later.

Two Countries Divided by Geography

John Sheffield

"Have you been here before?" the elegant woman asked.

"No," I replied. This is my first time in India. You're British, aren't you?"

"English, actually. My husband and I...he's back there...live in Little Chumley. It's near Stow-on the-Wold."

"I took a tour of the Cotswolds some years ago. Beautiful country. I remember Stow."

"Super."

"I don't think we went to Little, er...Chumley."

"I see. You take the Moreton road out of Stow, go left at the Wagon and Horses, and then right at the Plume. You can't miss it. We're the large house at the end of the village."

"I love the way you English use pubs to give directions."

"Jolly good. And you are from?"

"Outside Milwaukee."

"Ah, yes. Milwaukee. Super. Milwaukee.... I'm afraid my knowledge of American geography is a trifle sketchy."

"North of Chicago."

"I see. Chicago. Wonderful. I expect you enjoy it."

"Yes. We're not far from Lake Michigan."

"Great. So I suppose there's a lot of fishing and...er...cotton plantations."

"You're thinking of Mississippi."

"I am? Am I? So, you're not in the...er—"

"South. No, we're up north...Canada's even further up."

"Indeed. Good. Canada. Eskimos and the like. Super…Oh, we've stopped. I need to catch up with my husband. He's a real whiz at geography. I'm sure he knows all about Mississippi."

Warriors

Wars	Susan Crawford
Finally a Hero	Marty Aftewicz
Old Soldiers Never Die…	John Tabellione
The Lionhearted	Clayton H. Ramsey

Wars
Susan Crawford

You my old-souled warrior friend,
Written down in purple ink,
Fragmented in mid-page and charred,
Deserve some bit of rainbow glass, at least
A glimpse of a brown leaf from that first cold autumn.

How strange our brief encounter
Down in the green past
Brown eyes staring into screened-in summers,
Lemonade in circus glasses
And my dog friend silent in the road

This and something far more tragic,
Yet more precious,
Barely stirring in the dusty cardboard rooms.
A cup of rain
Reminds me somehow of that broken-winged bird
Buried with a twig cross
Behind the house
And of that night in a downtown room
When I first saw the rain
Behind your eyes and through my soul and here
To this small cup
Cracked partway up the red brick stairs to now.

Finally a Hero

Marty Aftewicz

Some visitors whispered words of prayer and encouragement, while others spoke of renewing old friendships at a less somber occasion. The mourners followed a common path as they entered the parlor then trudged toward the casket.

Three elderly men in the back of the room remained isolated for quite some time, appearing relaxed as they observed the procession. The widow spoke with them for just a few seconds when they arrived, but she'd not embraced them as she had most others.

The men's gaze locked on a young man who shared in greeting the guests. He was at that age when he was too old to be categorized as a young adult yet leaning to middle age all with one event.

The visitor voices together created a myriad of tones that frayed that young man's nerves and echoed in his ears. He wanted to bolt from the room into the cool autumn air but held his ground. He represented his family now, and he knew his father was proud.

The band of men intrigued him, and he slipped away from the greeting line to meet the trio before they left. Their eyes followed him as he maneuvered a path to reach them.

"Hello, Robert." He grabbed the extended hand and was surprised by the strength in the grip of this aged gentleman.

"I apologize, but I don't remember—,"

"I'm Lug. We're friends of your father."

 Robert noticed the use of present tense and had admonished himself numerous times in the past few days for the same mistake.

"I hope you don't mind us sitting back here waiting for the crowd to thin. Clutch here," Lug nodded, "he don't do real well in crowds with his oxygen tank and all. Besides, he's a bit self-conscious about this stainless steel horse he's strapped into."

Clutch wheezed, "I…am…not." Each word was interrupted by a rapid shallow breath. "It's just…that you…can't…drive." He peered up from the chair as if searching for validation. "Lug guides…this…wheelchair…and uses…my feet as…bumpers."

The final man of the trio interjected, "Well, I'm Sparky." His handshake matched his appearance, frail and unsteady. "Please don't take my friends seriously, Robert. They've been arguing since 1942 and neither one has made a valid point yet. That's forty-five years of bullshit."

"Gentlemen, I'm very glad you came." Robert returned to his insulated greeting of the past few hours.

Sparky continued, "Lug here is nearly blind, but he's the only one with the strength left to push Clutch in his chair. And Clutch, well he really doesn't need that chair. I mean, he's no cripple or anything. He only has one lung and just can't catch a deep breath."

"And we couldn't come without Sparky," Lug interjected. "He insisted on driving." He grinned at his slight barb. "But Sparky missed his damn treatment 'cause Clutch didn't trust me to drive."

"You can't…even see…a wall. How…could you…drive…five-hundred…miles?"

This was quite the group. Robert was certain he would have remembered them if he had met them before.

"I can guide the wheelchair through the crowd if you gentlemen would like to pay your respects now," Robert offered.

The trio glanced at one another before Sparky explained. "Actually, we would appreciate it if we could wait 'til there were fewer people around. It's just that we have something we want to do for Axle. It's a ceremony of sorts."

Axle. Robert hadn't heard his father called that name since he was a young boy. Only his very oldest friends knew his dad by that reference.

"You knew my father during the war."

They each nodded without a word and their eyes shimmered.

"We served in the same platoon. We were in—."

Robert interrupted. "Same platoon, Jesus. I know who you guys are now. You were in the POW camp with my dad."

He knew his father had been a POW for twenty-eight months during World War II, but always refused to speak of his imprisonment. This reminded Robert of his father's nightmares, and how the angry wails would wake him when he was a child. He would then find his father sitting in a cold sweat on his favorite chair as he stared into oblivion. The only relief that Robert could offer was a game of gin rummy at 3 A.M., but the source of his father's anguish was never disclosed.

Robert blocked the movements and sounds of the entire room as he focused on the vacant years of his father's past.

Sparky continued. "Yeah, your dad was Axle. Back then, we all had nicknames and we were sort of fond of automobiles. So when we landed in North Africa, we assigned parts of cars to each other as nicknames, and they stuck. It was Axle's idea. Just another thing we owe him."

"How did you know he passed away? I never knew who you were, so I didn't call you." Robert said.

Sparky replied. "Well, we kept in touch with your mom. We actually met you back when you were a little tyke, maybe five or six. Your mother never cared for us too much. She said that after we would speak with your dad, his nightmares would get worse for awhile. And then when he had his stroke and couldn't talk, well, we just wrote letters."

Clutch raised his arm at the elbow as a sign to interject. "We…owe our lives…to Axle."

The trio took a moment to gaze at each other, and Lug nodded back at Sparky, who continued. "Your father was hero. Did you know that?"

Robert remembered his dad. "I knew he got quite a few medals, but he never shared their history. But yeah, he was a hero to me."

Lug's bass voice projected authority. "Did he ever tell you what he did? How he got us out?"

That was a mystery that Robert could never convince his father to reveal. His mother had just told him he escaped from a POW camp, and that's why he had nightmares. That didn't give enough detail to Robert, and his father would only say, make sense, "Maybe someday when you get older, I'll explain it to you."

That day never came, and Robert learned this history was simply too painful for his dad to discuss. He finally stopped asking.

Sparky continued, "We were in Stalag IIIB in Fuerstenberg, not far from Berlin in earl 1945. We knew our side was making progress towards winning the war because the Red Cross no longer was permitted to visit. The guards were becoming more aggressive and took out their anger on the most weak and helpless. Conditions were bad."

Clutch shifted in his chair and dabbed at his eye. Lug patted his shoulder and nodded again towards Sparky.

"We heard artillery in the distance. The next day, about half the guards were called to the front. Prisoners were dying every day, and burial detail was our exercise. We hadn't been fed for seven days and existed on a small stash of food we had secreted over time."

Robert stood riveted to Sparky's words as the reasons for his father's nightmares were untangled.

"One morning, we woke and half the barracks were empty, and another half of the remaining guards were gone as well. We were told the prisoners were being moved to another Stalag which had food and supplies, but we didn't believe it. You need to know that we were all in very bad shape. We were so weak we didn't think we could make the march to another Stalag, even if that story was true."

"Axle shook us before dawn and ordered us out of our bunks. He was covered with blood and had the eyes of a madman. We figured we were dead anyhow, so we followed him. He guided us outside to the rear of the barracks and we hid in the shadows."

Lug said, "We didn't know the plan. Axle wouldn't say anything. He just stared at the guard towers."

"I thought you wanted *me* to tell this story, Lug." Sparky said as he frowned, then continued.

"As I was saying, we were scared and confused. We were almost afraid of Axle. We'd never seen him with that look before. Clutch told Axle we were waiting for nothing; that the guards would change soon and then they would probably start our march. Axle just glared at Clutch and murmured, 'The guards ain't getting relieved.' At the hint of first light Axle handed us a set of keys and an envelope he had tucked in his pants. He told us to wait and slipped away. We watched the guard towers as the Nazis paced, expecting their morning replacements. A single shot sent chills through us. A moment later, your father burst around the corner and grabbed me and started dragging me. Lug hoisted Clutch over his shoulder and followed. One German soldier lay crumpled against the sidewall of the barracks, and another was slumped over the guard tower. Your dad had slit the throat of the guard that came down from the tower to check on their replacements, and then he took that guard's rifle and shot the other guard in the tower. We had the damn keys to the main gates and walked right out."

"Wasn"t…quite that…simple." Clutch gasped his critique of Sparky's rendition.

"Pretty much. The remaining guards were as stunned as we were, and probably expected an alarm and the morning shift to rush from their HQ any second. That never happened. By the time they started shooting, we were almost to the woods."

Robert sat and started to process these rather unbelievable words. The enigma of the nightmares had been revealed.

"Thanks, guys. I never knew. This explains a lot about my dad, especially his nightmares."

Lug bent his tall frame and whispered into my ear. "That's not the whole story, just yet."

Robert lifted his head and noticed the clouds that were enveloping Lug's eyes, as Sparky rested his brittle self next to the young man and continued.

"We were out, but had nowhere to go. We quickly realized that we probably just hastened our own deaths. We had no shoes, little clothing and faced a snow-covered forest behind enemy lines. Axle explained the envelope contained our Stalag IDs and told us to huddle together in the brush. The ID papers would identify us as American POWs and not spies or escaped Jews. He tossed the rifle into the woods and told us to forget it. If the

Germans found us they would shoot us for certain if we were armed. And then he just walked off. We never learned how he had taken out the three or four Krauts that were sleeping at the headquarters barracks, but it was obvious that's exactly why they didn't relieve the morning guard."

"About mid-day we heard a peculiar jingle of a bell and Axle coasted in on a bicycle with a young boy riding the handlebars. Axle had this shit-eatin' grin on his face, and the demons were gone from his eyes. Your dad''s feet were a bloody mess, but he didn't seem to care. The boy didn't speak English except for one word, 'chocolate'. Axle gave us two woolen blankets and promised he would return soon. Even with the blankets, we didn't know if we would survive another night. The German lad didn't seem bothered by the cold. He roamed and played in the woods but kept us within sight. Every so often he would come near us and smile like he knew something we didn't, then would just say, 'chocolate'. We hadn't eaten for nine days and this kid was jumping about singing chocolate every few minutes. We heard the sounds of a distant battle but had little expectation of being found alive by friendly forces. Just before dusk, we heard approaching motors. Our young German friend hopped about the forest, repeating 'chocolate, chocolate'. As we peered through the brush, there came Axle riding with a platoon of Russian soldiers and a medic wagon. The German boy showed no fear and was clapping his hands as he rushed towards Axle, who proudly paid the bicycle rental with a huge handful of chocolate bars."

"Can I speak now, Spark?" asked Lug.

Sparky went silent.

"A few days later, the Russians liberated Stalag IIIB. We wanted to report Axle's actions to our guys when we were handed over. You know, he was a real hero; deserved the Silver Star at least. But he wouldn't hear of it. He got real agitated and got this spaced-out look and said, 'Those guys we buried back at camp, they were heroes. We're just doing our job. We're not heroes, yet."

"We never spoke of what he did until today."

A reverent silence captured the group. Robert held his father in even greater admiration after learning of these heroics. He then recalled the request by these three men to pay a tribute to their companion, and he extended his arm toward the front of the room. Just about everyone had left the funeral home except for the widow and a few close family friends.

The trio aligned themselves parallel to the casket and Lug helped Clutch to his feet. A few minutes passed while Clutch caught his breath from this mild exertion. They each withdrew small metallic objects from their pockets. As Lug and Sparky rested their items in the casket, Robert recognized the shape of a large gold star with a tiny silver star superimposed in the center - the Medal of the Silver Star.

Sparky and Lug spoke in unison, "For Gallantry in Action."

Clutch leaned over and placed a third Silver Star across Axle's chest.

"Finally…a hero."

Old Soldiers Never Die...

John Tabellione

The contrast of the dazzling springtime sun against Marietta's azure morning sky creates a frame over the twenty-three rolling acres of the Georgia National Cemetery. Treed with majestic, leafy oaks and magnolias, sporting magnificent bouquets of pure white blossoms, together they form a natural canopy of shade on a daily vigil; a scene, painters can only hope to capture and emulate in still life.

This silent setting allows me to bear witness to a reverent ceremony about to begin. It will serve as blessing before a meal for tens of thousands of picnics held on this day from Charleston to Carlsbad, Minneapolis to Indianapolis, and from Marietta, Ohio to its namesake city here in Georgia. Practically every one of these backyard barbecues will reflect a similar scenario. However, legions of military veterans won't be able to make it today, yet it is their lives everyone is honoring. You see, these cookouts are not for birthdays, but for end days: it is Memorial Day they are celebrating.

As a sponsor since 1988, the Knights of Columbus have again committed this year to organizing a memorial Mass. Momentarily, the faithful will begin to participate in prayer to remember the souls of more than seventeen-thousand fallen warriors who now rest in peace.

When I first became aware that the Knights have nearly two million members worldwide, I began to comprehend how the world's largest Catholic fraternal organization has the resources to perform millions of volunteer service hours, and has been able to contribute billions of dollars to charity over the course of the past ten years. The Knights have also proudly built a reputation for providing active support to members of the U.S. armed forces and their families throughout their 130-year history, and they continue to do so during the current world conflicts.Recently, they established a $1 million scholarship on behalf of the Archdiocese for the Military Services, USA, to help fund education for seminarians preparing to become Catholic chaplains in the U.S. branches of service.

I learned that these men they call Knights come from the Bishop Charles P. Greco Assembly #2161, which represents five local churches: Holy Family, St. Ann, St. Joseph, St. Peter Chanel and St. Thomas. I recall watching as each church was built, over the past several decades, and when their respective KofC Councils were established. But I digress.

Today the Most Reverend Wilton D. Gregory, Archbishop of Atlanta, has driven here to celebrate a commemorative Mass. I focus on His Excellency's entrance as a contingent of a dozen Knights of the Fourth Degree—the highest rank or "Patriotic" degree of the order—march as an honor guard. They escort him to the altar set up on the spacious, marble-columned rostrum overlooking the cemetery. Another little known fact I have discovered is that Archbishop Gregory's birthday coincidentally falls on Pearl Harbor Day, December, 7th. Few people know that the Pearl Harbor Survivors Association erected a monument here, on the 55th anniversary of this infamous date. But I do. I was here on that occasion, too, when they dedicated it in 1996. Trust me, I know a lot about these hallowed grounds, but hardly anyone knows who I am.

The Knights' regalia feature illustrious, plumed chapeaus and pressed tuxedos; the men shoulder a variety of capes in green, crimson, purple, gold or white. In addition, they wear red, white and blue striped service baldrics to hold their ceremonial swords and scabbards. Four of their brothers bear flags to form a color guard and initiate the posting of the colors while the *National Anthem* is played and sung. As I monitor from afar, I silently salute their military bearing and aplomb.

Volunteers have arranged several long rows of folding chairs beside a path in front of the rostrum. They will be occupied by VFW and American Legion veterans, young families, retirees, current service men and women in uniform, and members from said respective churches. The Archbishop, the Knights, several priests and a few dignitaries sit ensconced, meanwhile, on the covered stage which is draped in red, white and blue bunting.

I sense the attendees' somber respect while they are present in this sacred venue. I also notice they listen attentively to the head of the Atlanta Archdiocese as he proceeds to celebrate Mass and again later, as he offes a homily of gratitude to the deceased veterans.

Another group of six men from St. Ann's parish—"The Noteable Knights"—gather on a swath of grass toward the side of the high altar. They stand at attention in their uniforms of navy blazers, crisp white shirts, red ties, and grey slacks. Accompanied by a keyboardist, they lead the congregation in several appropriate hymns: the comfort of *The 23rd Psalm;* God's majesty in *How Great Thou Art*; and—following a solo trumpeter playing *Taps* amid the stillness at the end of the Mass—the pride inherent in *God Bless America* as the Archbishop and his honor guard exit in procession.

The crowd slowly disperses to socialize with each other in small groups, having paid their respects and thanks to those buried here. They will soon join their family and friends at picnics where toddlers will blow bubbles and waddle to catch them before they pop. Older kids will wave miniature American flags and chase each other. Some may play catch, or try to fly a kite. Adults may choose to chat about baseball scores, the fickle weather, even politics. The cookouts create an aura of good times for everyone, even though the guests of honor will never appear.

Before he departs, I observe Archbishop Gregory pausing for photos with the Knights while another type of changing of the guard occurs. Several military personnel man the driveways and paths leading from the cemetery's archway and wrought iron gates—an entrance of monumental masonry supported by a pair of Doric columns. They are preparing for an armed forces civil remembrance service in the next hour.

The symbolism of these twin events is not lost on me as a deceased serviceman. I recognize and have great faith in what my Savior has done for me by dying on the Cross. I truly understand what it means to have no greater love than to lay down one's life for another. In the case of the sacrifice of those buried here, it was for our country, so that subsequent generations of citizens could live here in freedom, practice their respective faiths and enjoy their pursuit of happiness—including the carefree fun and food at Memorial Day gatherings.

On behalf of all of my fallen brothers and sisters, I want to say "thank you" to everyone, especially the Knights of Columbus, for remembering us on this commemorative occasion today. I implore you to please return with families, friends and neighbors next year and for all of the years thereafter *in memoriam*. Even though I am unable bodily to attend any of those picnics, held in my honor and in honor of my fellow soldiers, marines, airmen, and sailors, know that our legacy will always stand with you in spirit.

May God bless America.

The Lionhearted

Clayton H. Ramsey

The sky was a cornflower blue, unmarred by clouds, the day Peter came back from Korea. He was a genuine, all-American war hero, with a chest full of medals to prove it. Even the weather seemed custom-made to celebrate his arrival at the docks in San Francisco Bay. As he lumbered down the gangway of the troop transport ship, shouldering his duffel bag, his parents, brother, and sister strained to see him among his fellow Marines. They shielded their eyes from the mid-day sun, pointing, searching, with anticipation nearly explosive after two years of letters and prayers and hoping for his safe return.

"There he is!" his mother, Claire, shouted.

She thought she had seen him three times before, and finally she was right. There he was—strong jaw, muscular build, a head taller than his companions, dark, penetrating eyes that seemed to stare to the horizon. His left leg dragged with a slight limp. That was new. He had mentioned something in his last letter about being wounded, but provided no details. The postmark was from a military hospital in Seoul. He said he would tell them about it when he returned.

"He looks thin," his mother said. "But he looks good." She raised a lace handkerchief to her mouth, tears rolling down her cheeks, unable to look away.

"Yep, he sure does," his father, Ben, said, flicking at the corner of his eye, swallowing the tremble in his voice.

At the end of the gangway, the single file of men in khaki fanned out into the screaming crowd. Camera bulbs popped, American flags waved, signs of love and welcome, hand painted in bold letters, were thrust above hats and arms. It was a mass of celebration, electric with emotion, crackling with tears and shouts of joy. The noise of weeping and laughter nearly drowned out a brass band that played at the edge of the dock. There were streamers and confetti, banners and balloons in myriad variations of red, white, and blue — a fitting welcome for the young men who had risked life and limb to stop the Red Menace on the Korean Peninsula, protecting the freedoms and way of life of the God-fearing nation of the good ole U.S. of A. Men had come back from war for thousands of years, and yet this day was uniquely American, wrapped in the Stars and Stripes and accompanied by the music of John Philips Sousa. Corn-fed Iowa farm boys and streetwise Brooklyn toughs, and young men from every city and town in between, had answered the call to serve and consequently been changed by the horrors of war. They were wounded and scarred, some crippled with battle fatigue, most simply tired of the fighting. But today, those who fought and survived were all welcomed as heroes, a tribute to their God, their Corps, and their country.

In a swarm of people so large and so frenzied, the possibility of reunion seemed remote, for one person to find his family among thousands. But Peter's head stuck up above the rest and his mother followed his military cap as it bobbed and ducked around kissing couples, wives hugging husbands, and small children hanging on the legs of long absent fathers.

She dug her nails into her husband's forearm, her gaze riveted on that tall son of hers, and pulled the rest of her family forward, planning to meet Peter as he looked for them. Pushing through the hundreds of little reunions that divided the crowd, Claire drove ahead to shorten the distance between them. Finally, in a nearly cinematic way, the clogged path opened and Peter stood in front of his family, wild with happiness. He dropped his bag and threw his arms first around his mother, who dissolved in his embrace. Ben wrapped his arms around both of them.

His sister, Marie, squealed with delight, and younger brother, Leon, unable to encircle the huddle, slapped his brother on the back. Normally a polite family, they all talked at once.

Claire couldn't stop crying and saying, "You're home, you're finally home. I love you, Peter. I love you so much."

Ben, usually stoically silent, only said, "Glad you're back, son."

Marie, still a teenager, giggled and jumped up and down in her black and white saddle Oxfords, her favorite poodle skirt dancing along. "Peter, Peter, Peter," was all she could squeak out.

Leon, a couple of years younger than his twenty-six-year-old brother, beamed. "Welcome back, Peter."

They stood there, crying and hugging, no one really believing that the gangly boy who left them was the man who was with them again. For his family, it was inconceivable that he could disappear for a few years into a dangerous, far-away place and return relatively unharmed. For him, it was nothing short of a miracle that he could survive blood-freezing cold, unending mud, hordes of Chinese Communists and the Korean People's Army soldiers that poured like swarms of insects across battlefields. Only his father, who had been gassed but survived action around Ypres in the final days of the First World War, knew what he had endured. The others could only imagine. They were simply happy to be together again.

The drive home in the surf green Chevrolet Townsman station wagon with wood trim and wide white walls was awkward. The thrill of the reunion had settled into the realization that Peter was no longer just a memory, a phantom family member recalled tenderly. Now he was here, in the toughened flesh, and beyond expressing their love and gratitude for his presence, they were at a loss for what to say. How did his family recount two years of missed birthdays, broken hearts, business deals, and church socials? And how did he tell them about what he had seen and felt without terrifying them with the nightmare he relived every night?

So, at an impasse, they rode in silence until Claire said, "Peggy asks about you every time I get groceries. You know she's a cashier at the Safeway, don't you?"

"Well, no, I…" Peter replied.

"No," Claire said, blushing, "Of course you don't. Well, she is and I think she's a little sweet on you. I know she'll be glad to see you."

"Now, Claire, he's not home an hour before you're trying to marry him off," Ben said.

"Oh hush. I'm just telling him what he's missed and who missed him. That's all."

"I made the cheerleading team, Peter!" Marie said.

"Great, Sweet Pea! That's just super," Peter replied. "And how have you been, Leon?"

His brother, staring out the window, turned to face his brother. "Okay, I guess. Things are busy at the store. Nothing to speak of."

Leon had always lived in his brother's shadow, both physically and metaphorically. Whereas Peter was massive, a football and basketball star in high school, Leon was scrawny, "delicate," his mother would say. With a slight scoliosis, flat feet, and poor vision, Leon was not attractive either to the athletic department at their school or to the draft board of the United States Army. Declared a 4F, "Unfit for Duty Due to Medical Reasons" scrawled in his chart, he was dismissed from consideration, even as his brother joined the Marine Corps to much fanfare and praise. While Peter was winning medals for bravery, Leon was assistant manager at the local Sears. It was a good job, steady, but nothing compared to the glory his older brother was earning on the battlefield. He read his brother's letters, joined his father's prayers before meals for his brother's safety, imagined what it must be like to face death every day, but his emotions were divided. He loved his brother, hoped he would return, prayed he would not be shot dead in some foreign country, but he also envied his brother's talent and strength, jealous of his courage, and wished it could be him dodging fire and vanquishing enemies. His brother had always gotten the attention for his athletic and academic abilities. He got the dreamy looks of girls, the praise of teachers, and the admiration of coaches. He was always the favorite, and now he was back, this time awash in the applause of a nation. Leon was happy and jealous, relieved and resentful. He didn't know what to think, what to feel. So he let the others do the talking.

Claire had prepared for days for Peter's return and when Ben unlocked the front door of the house and it swung open, the house glistened in greeting, smelling of Pine Sol and fresh linen. A huge banner was stretched across the foyer: "Welcome Home, Peter!" A cake waited on the dining room table under glass, and there were cups and plates placed beside a crystal punch bowl.

"I've invited a few folks over, Peter. I hope you don't mind," Claire said, almost apologetically. "Everybody is so eager to see you."

By the time he had dropped his duffel in his old room and washed his face, neighbors were already filtering into their home, anxious to lay eyes on a war hero and hear his stories. They came with food and gifts. Most remembered welcoming brothers, sons, and fathers home a decade ago from Europe and the Pacific, and they knew what they must do to express their appreciation to Peter and celebrate his homecoming. A little like a startled groom at his wedding reception, he stood, wide-eyed and smiling, in the parlor, shaking hands, giving hugs, accepting thanks, and dispensing innocuous bits of information about the war, always ending on a positive and patriotic note. After several hours of this, Claire noticed the weariness in Peter's eyes and nudged the remaining guests out the door.

Without reveille, Peter slept until 9 a.m. the next morning, an unheard of luxury. Ben had left hours before for his office, and Leon had been up and out by dawn, required to open the store, as he did six days a week every week of the year. Used to K rations, Peter inhaled the ham and cheese omelet and buttermilk biscuits his mother put in front of him. As long as she cooked, he ate, both ecstatic in their once familiar roles.

He had hoped for at least a day to read a book in the hammock, strung between birch trees out back, to go for a walk, drop a fishing line in the pond. He considered paying Peggy a social call, but by the time his mother was washing his breakfast dishes, a newspaper reporter knocked on the front door.

"Pardon me, ma'am," the man said, doffing his hat when Claire, drying her hands on her apron, met him at the door.

"May I help you?"

"Yes, ma'am, I hope you can," he said. "Is this the home of Captain Peter Lowry?"

"Yes," she answered tentatively.

"My name is Frank McCord, and I'm from the *Los Angeles Times*. I understand that Captain Lowry won a Distinguished Service Cross in Korea—a DSC, they call it--among other awards for gallantry. We'd like to do a story on him. You know, local man returns a hero. That sort of thing."

Color rose in Claire's cheeks without her effort. "Distinguished what?"

"Distinguished Service Cross, ma'am," he said. "It's our nation's second highest award for bravery. The only award more coveted is—"

"The Congressional Medal of Honor," Peter finished the reporter's thought as he rounded the corner from the kitchen. "Good morning. I'm Captain Lowry." He stuck out his hand.

The newspaperman shifted his hat and pad to his other hand and met Peter's. "It's an honor, sir. A real honor."

Peter smiled. "What can I do for you?"

"How about a few minutes of your time? We'd like to do a story on you for the *LA Times*, if you are agreeable."

Peter rubbed the back of his neck and looked over at his mother, who shrugged. "I know you're not one to brag, son, but it might help other families to know what you did over there."

Peter nodded and pointed to the parlor and both men found a place to sit.

"Can I bring you something to drink, Mr. McCord. Coffee? Tea? Anything for you, Peter?"

"Just some— "Peter started.

"Coffee is fine," the reporter cut in.

"--water, mother," Peter said, smiling. "Thanks."

After they had both settled into their seats, the reporter dove into his long list of questions, asking everything from what his favorite classes were in high school to what his father did for a living, scribbling the answers in his notebook. What he really came for, though, was The Story, the details of what Peter had done to earn his medals, especially the DSC.

"Not much to it, really," Peter began modestly. "It was a bitterly cold day, as most days over there were, and we were moving along a mountain pass, my buddy Steve at point. Suddenly the whole world erupted in flame, machine gun fire and grenades coming from all around us. Steve was the first to go down. I didn't have time to think. I pulled him to safety and yelled for everyone else to take cover. While my company was pinned down, and even though I was injured, I took out one machine gun nest of Chinese nationals, and then a second one on the other side of the pass."

"By yourself?"

Peter nodded.

"My God. You do deserve a medal," the man said. "Why not the Medal of Honor?"

"Since most are given posthumously, I'm happy my superiors gave me what they did. Either way, it's a privilege of a lifetime for any soldier."

"That it is, son," the man said. "Now I just have a few more questions for you…"

After an hour-and-a-half answering questions and a few that were not on his list, Peter politely withdrew from the conversation and escorted the reporter to the door, each thanking the other for the privilege. The rest of the day was busy. A small group from the Chamber of Commerce came by to talk about plans to host a parade in Peter's honor, followed by a steady stream of friends and neighbors who dropped in to welcome him back, verifying he was all right, and filling him in on what he had missed.

After almost a full day of hugging and listening to stories about prize-winning rhubarb pies at the county fair, Jake Tomlinson running around on his wife, dozens of babies being born, the new street lights being installed downtown, and hundreds of other details of a life that had gone on without him while he was overseas, he was thoroughly exhausted. He decided to go for a walk, get away from people for a few minutes. But every step he took, heads turned. Mothers presented their babies to him for a kiss from a genuine, home grown hero. Men gave him vigorous handshakes and told him how proud they were of him.

He finally ducked in O'Terry's Bar, but was no less anonymous there. When the bartender realized who he was, he told Peter his drinks were on the house for the rest of his life.

"For what this young man did for our boys over there, it's the least I could do," the bartender told the regulars.

With drinking come stories and the broken down men saturated with alcohol pressed him for tales of his heroism, hoping to infuse themselves with some measure of his strength and manhood. And so he told *The Story*. Again. It wouldn't be the last time. The men, rheumy eyed and slack jawed, stared in amazement, imagining how a man that had done something superhuman like that could be sitting with them in their dim, smoky bar on a Tuesday afternoon. When he finished, they actually clapped for him, some even wiping their eyes--a true hero in their midst. He thanked the bartender for the drink and the men for their time and stepped back onto the sidewalk, shading his eyes.

It was a short stroll back to the house. Claire had dinner waiting for him when he returned—little new potatoes with a butter glaze, Porterhouse steaks, salad with fresh vegetables from the garden, biscuits, green beans, Jell-O with bits of canned fruit suspended in the shimmering middle, corn on the cob.

"Nothing's too good for your first real dinner home," she said.

Leon was a few minutes late. He was required to close up at the end of the day. They were a little more relaxed than they had been alone with Peter the previous day. Claire mentioned the reporter, which was followed by questions and a recital of *The Story*. Suddenly Marie's struggles with algebra and Ben's disagreement with one of his subordinates didn't seem quite so important. All of them wanted to know more. How many Chinese soldiers were there? Did his friend survive? How did he fight off so many enemy soldiers when he was wounded?

He patiently answered their questions. His mother beamed with pride in her brave son and his father nodded quietly.

"Isn't that amazing, Leon?" his mother asked. "Isn't your brother simply amazing? And to think he's a part of this family."

Leon had been staring at his food as he lifted one forkful after another to his mouth. When his mother directed the attention to him, he slowly looked up at her, then at Peter, and then back at her.

"Yes, mother, he's an incredible guy," he said, his gaze returning to his dinner.

The rest of the meal was filled with small talk as Peter tried to divert the conversation onto other topics: his father's job, his sister's social life, his mother's sewing circle. Everyone knew Leon's life was just twelve-hour days at the department store and nothing more. He had few friends, no hobbies, no time for anything other than inventory, ledgers, and shopper complaints. So the discussion went around him, like a fast moving creek around a stone. He didn't mind; he was tired and wanted to finish his dinner.

After the meal, Claire cleaned up, Ben went to listen to the game, Marie sprinted upstairs to write in her diary about her brother's exploits, and Peter decided to relax on the porch swing. Leon joined him.

"Hey, little brother," Peter said as Leon slid into a white wicker chair beside the swing. It was a hot, sticky night and the only sounds were the whir of cicadas and the creak of Peter's swing. Neither should have had any worries. Peter was safe at home, not in a foxhole dodging bullets, and Leon was the assistant manager of a successful department store during the boom years of mid-century America. Both were lost in anxious thought, Peter about the look in the eyes of the refugees he saw beside the roads in Korea, the stench of corpses, the waste, and Leon about a phone call he had received that afternoon.

"What was it like?" Leon finally said, breaking the silence.

"Did you ever read Dante with Mrs. Willingham?"

"Yeah," Leon said, confused. "We all did in eleventh grade."

"Do you remember Cocytus in the ninth circle of hell, the frozen lake in the center of the Inferno?"

"Where traitors and Satan himself were trapped in ice?"

"It was like that," Peter said with a faraway look. "Cold, abysmally cold all the time, winds tearing at your skin like filleting knives. You could hardly feel your fingers to hold your rifle, much less pull the trigger. Always hungry, numb, exhausted, terrified. It was the fear that was the worst, constantly wondering if you could stand the pain if you stepped on a landmine, what it was like to die."

Both sat for a moment as the words settled between them.

"I think about that, too," Leon said softly.

"Don't you worry about it. I'm back home now. I didn't die."

A melancholy smile snuck up on Leon's lips. "I'm glad," he said. "No, I mean about me."

"About you?" Peter asked with concern.

Leon stared straight at him. "I have cancer. The doctor called this afternoon."

A profound silence pooled between them, as everything--insects, the tree frogs, the house, the world itself--stopped, the universe a still point paused by these two short sentences. Peter's eyes widened as he realized the specter of Death he thought he had outwitted in Korea had been waiting for him at home all the time.

"My God, Leon, why didn't you say something? Do mother and father know?"

"No, they don't. Not yet. Everyone just seemed so excited you were home, the big war hero, that I didn't want to ruin the mood with my news." His eyes seemed to pull back into dark sockets in his skull, and suddenly Leon was not the little kid anymore, always tagging after his older brother, looking up at him with affection and admiration; he was an old man, limping to the grave.

Peter, an ex-Marine for only a day, choked back tears, but the brother in him jumped up and threw his arms around Leon. He held his frail brother, his hug communicating in ways his words could not. When he finally let Leon go, his cheeks were slick and his muscles quivered with emotion. Leon sat very still. All he said was, "Thanks."

"Anything I can do?" Peter asked.

"Like shoot the tumors?"

"No, c'mon," he shifted uncomfortably. "You know, like is there anything I can get for you? How can I help you through this?"

"Well, right now I'm okay, just a little tired. Maybe later there might be some things you can help me with."

"Wh—what's the prognosis?" Peter asked.

"Doc Whittlesly gives me about two to four months to live."

"Anything they can do?"

"Not much," Leon said. "It's too advanced. They can give me some pills for the pain, but it's too late for surgery, and radiation is too expensive for us."

"You've got to tell our parents."

"I will, but I don't want to burden them. They're good people, and they suffered enough worrying about whether or not you would come home," Leon said, looking up at the pain in his brother's eyes. "Sorry. I don't want you to feel guilty. But it's the truth," he added.

"So you're just going to smile and pretend everything is all right?"

"Yeah, I am. The doctor told me what to expect as the cancer spreads, about the pain, about my body shutting down."

"Why do that alone? Don't you want others to know?"

"No, others have their own lives, their own worries. I'll just deal with it. There's nothing our parents can do about it anyway. Why not enjoy the time we have left? Plus, I won't be totally alone; you'll know and you can help."

"I don't understand—honestly, I don't--but I admire you and I've learned not to argue with you once your mind is made up." Peter gave him another hug and said, "I'm here. Always."

"I know. Thanks."

For the next couple of months, Peter was feted. There were parties for him, and he rode on the back of a red Cadillac convertible, with tricolor bunting on the bumper, as the honorary Grand Marshall of the 1954 Parade of Heroes, followed on floats by the Succotash Queen, a Life Scout who had pulled a boy from the river, and the Lion's Club Man of the Year. Men continued to buy him drinks, and there was even a proposal to name a street after him.

Leon went to the parade and the parties, as faithful as a little brother could be, and every time Peter saw him—waving a tiny American flag on the sidewalk with the rest of his family as Peter rode by waving to the crowd, or standing by the punch bowl at the VFW Lodge or the church Fellowship Hall during a party for Peter—a sharp stab of guilt skewered him. With every smile and every appearance, Peter was reminded of what Leon was suffering privately. Every time he saw his brother look for a chair or reach for something to steady himself, he knew the fatigue was creeping up on Leon. When he paused to catch his breath or pushed away a half eaten plate of food at the dinner table, Peter knew. A grimace or the green tint of nausea were constant evidence that his brother was dying and there was nothing he could do, except keep his secret and help as he could.

Since Leon had always been sickly, his parents were not particularly attentive to these new developments, especially since there were so many opportunities to celebrate the gallantry of their other son, the scholar-athlete and war hero. They barely noticed him spending more time in the bathroom, or his weight loss, or his increasing frailty. But Peter did, and he brought his brother medicine, watched after him as a guardian angel, as much out of guilt as out of love. Leon pushed through the pain, never giving any indication of what he was enduring.

One night at dinner, as the rest of the family enjoyed lasagna, thick with mozzarella and sauce made from fresh garden tomatoes, Peter caught Leon out of the corner of his eye, swaying slightly at his place. Without warning he pushed back from the table and stumbled to the bathroom down the hall, vomiting into the sink before he could reach the toilet.

"Leon must have picked up a virus somewhere, probably one of those customers at the store. Ben, go check on the boy," Claire said.

Ben did, followed closely by Peter. They both struggled to carry him to his bed. He was only 115 pounds, but he was absolutely limp, dead weight. Claire brought him some medicine for his stomach and a glass of ginger ale. Peter sat beside him as he slipped into unconsciousness. He stayed in that bed for three days. His mother thought it was the flu. When he died on the fourth day, his mother was beside herself. What could have happened? Why is my boy gone? Her grief in his loss was vastly disproportionate to the attention she showed him during his life. She was too busy focusing on her successful son. They were shocked to learn of Leon's cancer, and never discovered Peter knew. They just thought Leon was being difficult, not that he was trying to spare them pain.

The service at the First Methodist Church they attended infrequently was the following Saturday. It was not Leon's funeral; it was the memorial for "Peter's brother." The minister said some pleasant things about him, read Scripture, prayed. Flowers came from all over the city, even a reporter or two showed up to document this "tragedy in Captain Peter Lowry's family." The turnout was larger than what you would expect for the quiet assistant manager of the local Sears. But, of course, they were not there to honor this young man; they were there to console the town hero and his family.

At the end of the service, before the casket was sealed and rolled out of the sanctuary, there was a chance to view the body, to say one last goodbye. A line formed down the central aisle and most politely waited to pay their respects, more to be seen than out of any real reverence. When it was Peter's turn, he pulled his Distinguished Service Cross out of his suit pocket and slipped it in a fold in the white satin lining beside his brother.

He leaned over Leon's waxy grey ear and whispered, "You deserve this more than I do. I'm not as brave as everyone thinks I am. You're the real hero. I'll miss you, brother. Go in peace."

And with that, he straightened up, ramrod stiff, and right there snapped a salute to this unknown assistant manager and bravest man in the room.

MEMOIRS

Maxwell's Bite   **Jan Slimming**

Local Retiree Carves a Legacy: **John Tabellione**
Jack Weller aka "Mr. Chips"

Ghost Train   **John Sheffield**

Maxwell's Bite
Jan Slimming

ESCHEW NUGATORY REMUNERATION! They marched on Fleet Street. The placards shouted messages of intellectuals in dispute. Writers and editors wore their collective hearts on their sleeves. Now they had an avid supporter for their voices to be heard; the NUJ.

The National Union of Journalists (NUJ) originally enlisted newspaper employees: journalists, typesetters, and print machine operators, but now writers and editors of books and magazines were eligible to join. They demonstrated to assert their employment rights, to save and improve jobs and their livelihoods. It was an era when everyone wanted to be appreciated by management; in this case the wealthy press barons. Writers of newspapers, magazines, books, illustrators, page-layout designers, and anyone handling print materials, from galley and film to advance copies, were included, even if they were in sales. Fleet Street moguls were unprepared for the onslaught of unrest and collective bargaining. The demonstrators' fear was New Technology. The computer age was coming and all were aware of the consequences should this automated scourge take over. It was November 1978 and the Canadian owners of The Times newspaper had halted production; the Union disputes were seriously having an effect. The owner's action was unprecedented; it was the first time this world renowned daily newspaper had not been published, since 1788.

* * *

I can't remember the exact date I joined the NUJ. It was definitely something I never expected—to be part of *a Union.* And, coming from a relatively conservative background, leaning slightly to the left and working class, I never thought I would be part of George's Union. He was our next-door neighbor, Shop Floor FOC (Father of the Chapel), at the Daily Telegraph; unionist and argumentative, not the best person to have living next door. I imagined his placards always read "more pay, more pay, more pay," "strike, strike, strike,"—such was the greed of printers in the sixties and early seventies. Now, ten years later, I was no longer a child and he had retired; New Technology had become the enemy. Jobs were threatened in all spheres of the publishing and printing trades. Computers were not permitted for NUJ members; unions had control.

* * *

My foray into publishing began when I travelled to London, from the suburbs of south London, to interview in Fleet Street. I had high grades in English and Business Studies and applied for my second job in 1971; my first had been with a paint manufacturer. That April day, after negotiating the revolving door of the old Fleet Street building and riding its creaky lift to the fourth floor, I found myself in the dark Victorian office of a rather dumpy looking personnel manager. A pleasant woman I seem to remember, with auburn curly hair. She wanted to know if I could type. I was hired for the trade magazine division. "Start on Monday." I only met her once.

My new employer was the magazine publishing company, Benn Bros. Ltd. The firm had moved to sparkling new offices in Lyon Tower, Colliers Wood, just three miles from my home in Mitcham. Here the low cost of land and rents provided a brand-spanking-new, modern office building; a sixties-style monolith of dark grey slab, incorporating rows of rectangular windows, all the same height and width. I worked on the second floor in an airy open-plan office; the Subscription Department. Editorial was on the third floor and the fourth housed a Computer Room. Sometimes the elevator stopped there by mistake, if you happened to take the wrong lift. The alighting staff with security badges would quickly open the double doors opposite and one could see banks of sheet metal cabinets, dials, switches and wires. The mysterious new-age machines appeared to stretch for miles. There was an air of secrecy on this floor and its vast Computer Room. I once asked a young man "what happens in there?" His reply was not at all revealing but he confirmed "only authorized people could enter." When I asked why? He replied "Dust!" I later learned that if you even glimpsed the towering metal obelisks it was too much matter; alien dust was simply not permitted; skin cells created too much dander and computers might fail. "Crash" was the word they used.

'Fleet Street' had made its first move to the suburbs. The significance of this, however, was lost on me at the time. I was quite happy for a year—as long as I had my Walkman, an electric typewriter and a calculator—these inventions were new enough technology for me, back then.

But the lure of friends working in central London eventually led me to leave my parochial position, and the following spring I applied for temporary work at double the pay. "A chance not to be missed," they said. The move, however, was less rewarding after three months of boring administrative law or government positions. Moving from place to place to cover vacation or maternity leave, I never felt a sense of belonging. I decided to find a more stable, permanent job, and after a quick agency call to establish my credentials, I attended an interview in Poland Street, London, W1.

The hustle and bustle of Oxford Street was always enthralling. I felt excited to be part of this vibrant city. The smells, the atmosphere, the mingled cacophony of sounds; large red double-decker buses hummed from stop to stop carrying throngs of people, while black cabs swerved to pick up and drop off passengers. They were a mix of nationalities; some professional men in suits or women in high-heels, some with hats and expensive-looking faux fur stoles, mothers with children, or buskers with their musical instruments. Illicit traders shouted in the streets, trying to sell their wares; the contents of which they stuffed quickly into milk crates when they saw a policeman approaching. By comparison the Department stores were fascinating, well lit and shining; fashions were fast moving. Top Shop was my favorite. We all had money to spend. I loved the new yellow dress I had bought to wear with my bright red platform shoes with turquoise polka dots. Feeling fashionable and colorful I was now ready to attend the interview that, if successful, would pay even more. I was still very young, in my prime and more than confident.

    I took the Northern Line tube from Colliers Wood, via Tooting Broadway, to Stockwell where I changed underground trains to the new Victoria line. The clean silver metal capsules sped smartly and quietly from station to station. Only a slight whooshing noise could be heard, together with the clunk of the automatic sliding doors as the station master shouted "Mind the Doors." At my designated stop I jumped off the train and rode the long escalator to the top. I blended in with the other rush-hour types and tourists, and eventually stepped from the depths of London's underground into the bright morning sunshine of Oxford Street, W.1. It was 9am. My London map—The A-Z— indicated I should find Argyll Street at the back of the Palladium Theatre. A strong aroma of freshly ground coffee beans invaded my senses as I walked along the wet, freshly sprayed, passage of back entrances and tiny merchants selling newspapers, cigarettes, coffee, and cabbage. The shortcut led to Marlborough Street and the beautifully preserved fascia of Liberty's; an original London department store dating back to 1874—an icon with Shakespearean overtones. Traffic was sparse in the back streets; one could just hear the faint muffled sounds of the busses and black taxis a block away in Oxford Street. Heading east, I found Poland Street. The narrow pavements seemed to suck in the heat of the morning sunshine. The speckled rays exaggerate the dark green, dusty, window ledges of the established cottage industries that hid behind even dustier and dirtier windows of craftsmen, sewing shops, small printers, pubs and offices. St. Giles House, number 49-50 was my destination—The British Printing Corporation. This was bohemia, on the edge of Soho.

Stepping through the modern-looking doorway, an intimidating shrouded corridor, of dark pine, stretched before me. The low ceiling spotlights seemed to burn into my skull. Several, small, softly-illuminated display cases punctuated the paneled walls, offering dingy and random colored jackets of children's books, tombs of war and latest fiction titles. The passage was about fifty feet long and, as I pushed open the double doors at the end, I stepped into a chasm of yellow light. I had arrived.

The BPC receptionist, Sally, was tall with long flowing blonde hair, I thought she should have been a model. "Somebody will be down to collect you soon," she stated professionally. A few minutes later, making small talk in a friendlier tone, she said she liked my yellow dress and red shoes; at that point I felt she might become an instant friend—if I was hired. The 'somebody' appeared at the elevator door. She called my name and indicated to follow her back into the small elevator. Slowly we rose to the fourth floor. Her name was Miss Huff—the Personnel Director's assistant; I needed to complete a few forms. How different she seemed from the Benn Brother's personnel manager. Valerie was young and slender, with long dark flowing hair, reminiscent of Cleopatra. I already felt I would like to work here. After a while I was ushered into see Victor Broadribb, her Director. A distinct aroma of lavender water, blended with cigarettes, seemed to hover in his book-filled office; the tall, and portly, older man greeted me warmly. His immaculate silver-grey pin stripe suit matched his silver-grey hair and expertly trimmed beard. A purple handkerchief peeped out of his breast pocket. It matched the purple of his tie which, in turn, was fastened to his crisply laundered white shirt with a sparkling diamond tie pin. He, of course, had matching cuff links. "Dapper," I thought. Mesmerized by his sartorial elegance, and half-moon reading glasses as he peered over the top of the frames, I remember little of our conversation, but I guess he thought I was "OK" to progress to the next stage of the interview.

"Soon," said Valerie, "I will introduce you to the Production Manager." We returned to the small elevator and went to the second floor. Stepping out into another wood paneled corridor, we narrowly missed colliding with a woman in hair curlers as she ran from the ladies' restroom to a door opposite. I later discovered she was Supervisor of the switchboard. The girls in the hidden telephone room were a law unto themselves.

As we passed through another set of heavy fire doors, we entered a maze of publishing offices, a mish-mash of modern and old styles. Telephones rang intermittently. The rooms had half-glass walls, some had outside windows, but many had borrowed-light and relied on fluorescent lighting. There was a low hum of muffled editors' voices; shadows of people gesticulated behind frosted glass. I was introduced to the Production Manager whose office was about the size of a large rectangular bath tub. Stephen was tall with dark curly hair; older but still seemed quite young. I later found out he was only twenty-eight. He was head of production for Macdonald Educational, the children's illustrated book division of BPC's Macdonald & Co. Publishers.

"We're in exciting times," he said playfully; his eyes twinkled behind thick rimmed glasses.

More help was needed in their department of four and I was introduced to the others—Penny, Rosemary and Philip. Next I was shuffled off to the third floor to meet the Editorial Director—Peter Usborne. I heard the next day I'd got the job: "Start on Monday!" It was

September 2nd, 1972; little did I realize this would be my career, my university, and my life, for the most part.

As the youngest and 'the last one in' you make coffee for your boss and the others. I hated that part. I didn't think I was supposed to do those kinds of menial tasks. I was trained in far more superior matters. But I sucked it up, and settled into the routine of organizing my boss which is what he wanted. The first thing to change was my office. It was too small and so was his. Down came the frosted glass partition between us to create a larger, twelve by twelve, room. I insisted on the newest technology and it was provided. Of course, I made a few silly mistakes and they were the talk of the department…but I rode the humor and joined in. I knew they loved me really; I became a team player, the key I discovered, to employment longevity. They played hard and worked hard, and I joined in.

The first party was three weeks after I started at BPC. It was held at Peter Usborne's house in Islington, on September 24th, 1972. The launch of the Starters Series was predicted by all to be a magnificent educational success. It was. After the launch there was no looking back. I met everyone; all staff had been invited, about sixty people—from the mail clerk, to the junior Accounts Clerk, the editors, the sales department and the Chairman. The event was a great exercise in team building and we all continued to work hard; it was teamwork. In December the Christmas Party also had its rewards—at The Ritz! It was a phenomenal and joyous occasion. I loved London life and very quickly fell in love with everything about the publishing industry.

* * *

Our department continued to excel, and, after a year doubled in size. We now handled all foreign rights and co-productions. This was big business. As part of the British Printing Corporation funding was not a problem, as long as we had a plan and tried. We attended international book fairs, created new systems for reports, maximized profitable print runs and ran with success. We handled manuscripts, galleys, color-separated films and color proofs, sending them to almost every country around the world. These were heady times. By 1976 our department alone was bringing in twelve million pounds annually, in overseas rights and co-editions sales; all in addition to BPC's main business of printing and selling books in the English language.

But there was talk in Editorial. Computers were coming. How were these going to affect our jobs? Printers, color reproduction specialists, designers, and production departments joined editors in Chapels to prepare for collective bargaining. Management called these 'disputes', when negotiations became serious. Threats of walk-outs by key employees became part of everyday conversation. How could this be? Everyone had seemed to be so happy.

I was encouraged to join SOGAT (The Society of Graphical and Allied Trades). Everyone was joining a union. It was the thing to do. Workers rights, fair wages, and maternity leave. I wanted all those things. But ultimately, the NUJ was a better choice for me, I was told; I handled printing films and was eligible to join. Everyone else in the department joined and so did I, together with other young assistants, Lucille, Susan and Margaret.

By 1977, unrest in Fleet Street was reaching breaking point. We had moved from Poland Street to Holywell House, on Worship Street, EC1, just north of the banking industry, Lloyds of London and Liverpool Street Station. The upgraded accommodation provided new offices on the fourth and sixth floor. This building had plenty of tall and wide plate-glass windows. The blue-green building was not exceptionally high, but the London views and natural day-light were indeed luxuries. This was to be our new base. It was also home to our sister company, Waterlow & Sons, a pre-eminent BPC security printer as well as a printer of four-color books and magazines. But the buzz of Oxford Street had been replaced by the rigid and damp atmosphere of the City; the nagging effect of employee unrest increased—was our division's success about to be destroyed by the Union?

      Management tried. Stephen, my boss and NUJ member, would rescind his membership if there was 'serious action'. There was and he, and others, resigned. Reluctantly I carried on, encouraged by other union members, who were also my friends. I was if anything curious to see how organized disputes operated. As ours escalated, we were summoned to take part in a lunchtime march. This was arranged by Fleet Street chapters of other book, newspaper and magazine companies. Around that time we had also merged with another sister company who published part-work magazines; now we were called Macdonald Phoebus. It was hard to see which company was the winner in this arrangement, but the move was considered a cost saving exercise by BPC management. Their actions immediately provided another grievance for the NUJ.

      And so, now fully enveloped in the rituals of a trade union, we marched on Fleet Street. Aversion to new technology was still the main theme; jobs, it was certain, would be lost. All union members had to support the status quo. Progress in technology was not considered progress in the union's eyes. Working on any form of new technology was not permitted. Disaster was surely impending. Lucille and Margaret between them deciphered the words on one of the placards—ESCHEW NUGATORY REMUNERATION! "Shun worthless pay!" the young teachers-cum-editors shouted vehemently, over and over again, as we marched along Fleet Street.

* * *

Managing Directors of Macdonald & Jane's, Macdonald Educational and Phoebus fought for their positions. It seemed a losing battle for some because they knew of an underlying threat. The

Board Directors of the parent company, BPC, gave ultimatums with strict instructions to "sort out the problematical staff". They tried but the union proved to be stronger having moved to hold a sit-in. One hundred and sixty key staff responded, and the dining room on the sixth floor of Holywell House became Union occupied. I refused to join in, but was sympathetic to the cause. Fortunately, I had a vacation planned in Florida for two weeks; I felt I would not be involved immediately, if at all. Everything would be resolved by the time I returned, I thought.

The vacation in November 1978 was a wonderful hiatus, but when I returned the dispute had escalated and both sides were now entrenched. It was stalemate. Tom Boardman, Managing Director of my company, had resigned (or had been fired, we were never sure which), and now I had to be prepared to go on lunchtime picket duty. My boss encouraged me to support the editors because he could not. On the first day back I was sent to Macdonald & Jane's offices in Shepherd's Walk, and stood outside with picket placards which read: "Fair Pay," "No Redundancies." Board negotiations were going on inside. It was ridiculous; it was serious. The Managing Director of Jane's, Ronald Whiting, emerged, ashen-faced and destroyed. Shoulders hunched over in despair. He had also been fired. We didn't really understand what was going on, there were rumors, but we thought rather they lose their jobs than we lose ours. Two days, later my next lunchtime picket was at the BPC's head office in Great Queen Street. Our new Managing Director, Peter Morrison, former CFO of Phoebus, arrived with his chief editorial director, Nicholas Wright. They walked through our picket line and through the revolving doors. Seconds later Morrison returned.

"I thought you were with us." He smirked. His small shiny pink face stared up at me as I stood on the top step to the doorway. He had stepped down onto the pavement. Both of us were short but now his diminutive status was exaggerated by our positions.

"No," I said sarcastically, looking down at him. He swiftly ascended the steps and re-entered the building. A minute later he returned with Nicholas Wright as his witness, and formally fired me. That was it, I had been fired. None of us took it seriously, but we didn't know at that point how much was at stake.

I returned to the occupied sixth floor of Holywell House. After months of sitting on the fence, I was definitely one of the militant team now; I felt collective grievance was a good thing and agreed to cover a few shifts over the Christmas Holidays; two hours here and there, during our protracted occupation. The sit-in continued for another month, but here was little action; management had become eerily silent. Eventually I found myself on a night shift. It was Burn's Night, January 25th, 1979. We were to have Haggis, and was told that I would enjoy this memorable and teaching moment.

The unusual concoction of strange meat from animal body parts combined with a mixture of herbs and barley, stuffed into a sheep's stomach, did not appeal, in any way, to my palate. The strange meal was something I'd written about in one of my earlier Traditional Foods projects. My mother had attempted to cook one when I was young, but I hadn't fully experienced the rituals of traditional Scots before. Only once, at one minute past midnight on New Year's Day, my uncle decided First Footingwouldscare my mother if he visited our home with a piece of coal, a dram of whisky and a blackened face. The tradition predicted good luck and plenty for the coming year, as long as a tall dark stranger—bearing the essential gifts—was first to cross the threshold on January 1st.

Burn's Night celebrates the eighteenth century Scottish poet, Robert Burns, born January 25th, 1759. On this day, his birthday, many Scots prepare an annual supper, and use the occasion to read his poetry and remember the songs of the young "Robbie" Burns. He died on July 21st,

1796. It is alleged his death followed a dental extraction the previous winter, exacerbated by his regular habit of intemperance which aggravated a long-standing rheumatic heart condition. He was thirty-seven.

The Burn's Night NUJ Occupation was planned; we would each bring something; I chose red wine. There was at least one Scotsman in charge of the evening and he would lead the ceremony. The 'occupied' location, on the sixth floor, had been carefully planned to include small offices for union members to sleep, a conference room with kitchen, and separate toilet facilities. The arrangement was perfect for a long term dispute…, and parties. This particular night was, I believe, a Saturday. We could lock ourselves in for the weekend and not worry about management's intrusion. The Occupation had been peaceful, for the most part, and the original management had become sympathetic to our cause; they all wanted pay rises and assurances too. They respected our security lines and left us to collectively organize our members, meetings, negotiations and action.

For Burn's Night I was in charge of peeling potatoes and turnips; 'Haggis and Neeps' was on the menu, with 'tatties' (mashed potatoes) and shots of Glenfiddich. Mike DeLuca, the Scotsman, arrived with the pre-stuffed haggis, together with a traditional dagger, stuffed into his sock. John Davis bought the expensive whisky. Jenny Golden and Susan Mead provided dessert; others arrived with more wine and coffee. Our FOC was also there, Neil Tennant; he brought his elevated union position. We were delighted the young respected editor and musician, from Northumberland University, was in charge. He knew everything about organizing industrial disputes, hailing from the north.

We were about twenty, in total, that night, and after lengthy preparations, our feast was finally ready to be presented. We gathered around the former conference room table, large enough for all to be seated. The lights were turned off and the Scottish tradition began. Everyone was quiet.

In the low light that emanated from the kitchen we were asked to stand as someone took the cue to light two large candles on the table. The sound of bagpipes started to wail around the room. From a dark corner a Scotsman appeared in a kilt and full traditional Scottish attire. His platter was held high, and atop was a meaty mound fully encapsulated in a sheep's grey stomach lining. A cacophony of melodic highland sounds played as other servers trailed around the table; they carried bowls of vegetables and other accompaniments. I noticed Scotsman Mike still carried the small dagger in his white knee-length socks, the handle of which just brushed the hem of his kilt. He stopped at the head of the table, having made a complete circuit; someone turned off the bagpipes. It was then that he started to recite in an indecipherable dialect. It was the beginning of the Robbie Burns tradition:

'Address to a Haggis'

Fair fa' your honest, sonsie face,   (fa = fall, sonsie = jolly/cheerful)
Great chieftain o' the puddin-race!
Aboon them a' ye tak your place,   (aboon = above)
Painch, tripe, or thairm: (painch = paunch/stomach, thairm = intestine)
Weel are ye wordy o' a grace   (wordy = worthy)
As lang's my arm.

The groaning trencher there ye fill,
Your hurdies like a distant hill,   (hurdies = buttocks)
Your pin wad help to mend a mill
In time o' need,
While thro' your pores the dews distil
Like amber bead.
At this point Mike pulled the glinting dagger from his sock, and plunged it dramatically into the haggis.

His knife see rustic Labour dicht,   (dicht = wipe, here with the idea of sharpening)
An' cut you up wi' ready slicht,   (slicht = skill)
Trenching your gushing entrails bricht,

Like ony ditch;
And then, O what a glorious sicht,
Warm-reekin, rich!   (reekin = steaming)

At the words *An' cut you up wi' ready slicht*, he sliced open the sheep's stomach from end to end.

One would think the ceremony was over at the point, however, it wasn't. Mike went on to finish every line:

Then, horn for horn, they stretch an' strive:
Deil tak the hindmaist! on they drive, (deil = devil)
Till a' their weel-swall'd kytes belyve,   (swall'd = swollen, kytes = bellies, belyve = soon)
Are bent like drums;   (bent like = tight as)
Then auld Guidman, maist like to rive,   (auld Guidman = the man of the house, rive = tear, burst) "Bethankit" hums.

Is there that o're his French ragout
Or olio that wad staw a sow,   (olio = stew, from Spanish *olla*/stew pot, staw = make sick)
Or fricassee wad mak her spew
Wi' perfect scunner,   (scunner = disgust)
Looks down wi' sneering, scornfu' view
On sic a dinner?

Poor devil! see him ower his trash,
As feckless as a wither'd rash,
His spindle shank, a guid whip-lash,
His nieve a nit;   (nieve = fist, nit = nut, i.e. tiny)
Thro' bloody flood or field to dash,
O how unfit!

But mark the Rustic, haggis fed,
The trembling earth resounds his tread.
Clap in his wallie nieve a blade,   (wallie = mighty, nieve = fist)
He'll mak it whistle;
An' legs an' arms, an' heads will sned,   (sned = cut off)
Like taps o' thristle.   (thristle = thistle)

Ye Pow'rs wha mak mankind your care,
And dish them out their bill o' fare,
Auld Scotland wants nae skinkin ware   (skinkin ware = watery soup)
That jaups in luggies;   (jaups = slops about, luggies = two-handled bowls)

But, if ye wish her gratefu' prayer,
Gie her a haggis!

Somebody had poured wine into the glasses while we stood, trying to understand this obviously important tradition. We all toasted the haggis. "Good Health!" Good health to the haggis, I thought; poor thing it was obviously well and truly slaughtered at this point.

"Tatties anyone?" It was John who broke the silence.

The rest of the evening moved along nicely with each person telling a story. Nearly everyone smoked cigarettes. Except Mike and John who brought Cuban cigars; no doubt another Burn's Night tradition—for them.

Soon it was midnight and I slept on the floor in one of the offices. Susan Mead slept in the same room. Needless to say the floor was most uncomfortable; it was early Sunday morning before I went home for a proper sleep, in my own bed, in my comfortable home, in Wimbledon.

* * *

The following week saw more Union disruption. Management pleaded with the Chapel to return to work, but the national NUJ leaders and our negotiating committee stuck to their democratic brief. There was no backing down; no settlement, not unless there was a firm guarantee of jobs, pay structure, benefits and working conditions. Further sit-ins had occupied other BPC buildings, and more aggressive marches were organized. Whispers of an impending threat became more prominent: Robert Maxwell was making a bid for our company. BPC was now at its lowest ebb and our branch of the dispute had seriously caught the attention of the media. The idea of a possible take-over by a man who, in Parliament, had been denounced as "unfit to run a public company" was alarming for everyone, especially the city and the stock market.

It wasn't long before a lunchtime meeting of NUJ organizers encouraged ITN to visit our comfortable strike premises; Jon Snow was the fresh-faced TV reporter. He had recently made news himself as the fiancée of Anna Ford, ITN's news anchor. We all gathered to hear him interview Neil, the FOC and national NUJ leader, Gary Morton, from The Times dispute. That night we watched ourselves on TV. There was an uncomfortable prediction that our management might no longer be around. The rumors became stronger, and our management was on its knees. It was likely Maxwell would take over. Shares were at an all-time low. Top management would all soon be fired.

A few more weeks went by and we all wondered what was happening. Some protestors fell by the wayside—they went back to work or found other jobs—but early in March we were all called to a meeting in the basement of Macdonald & Jane's offices. A skeleton group of 'tough guys' stayed behind in Holywell House to repel any middle management from taking back our occupied space.

* * *

The basement of Jane's Yearbooks and Fighting Ships head office, in Shepherd's Walk, London N.1, was dark and dingy. About eighty people crammed into the staff lounge. It was hot and uncomfortable. After fifteen minutes, a rustle went through the crowd, "He's coming!"

The double doors opened and a posse of five men and a woman entered. Everyone was exceptionally quiet. Somebody dropped a notebook on the carpet and even that soft noise seemed to echo around the room. In the center of the posse an imposing specter appeared in an oversized, navy, cashmere Crombie. The man's large square head almost touched the ceiling; he had a thick black main of Brylcreemed hair. The daunting figure was Robert Maxwell. It was easy to see why he was often described as a killer whale. He dipped his head below the door and stood in front of us. His shoulders seemed to touch each side of the walls of the small alcove. He had squeezed into the space between the vending machine and door, the only place left for him to stand. The rest of the posse stood by the entrance and, thankfully, held the door open. The lack of air was becoming troublesome. Fortunately, most of us were sitting on chairs or on the floor and, as far as I know, nobody fainted.

"Good afternoon, Ladies and Gentleman." His voice boomed around the room. It was just before lunchtime and my lurching stomach rumbled loudly.

"There are times when one has to cut out the bad and regenerate with new," he continued, ignoring the loud sound of my digestion tract.

"This is that time. You are not all bad people; it is your management that is unable to manage or unwilling to negotiate terms to ensure employees are happy." We all smiled at this.

"From now on I will be in charge of running this company and will meet your officers to discuss your needs. The current Managing Directors will be leaving, and new managers, like yourselves, will be offered positions in my company. But, there are things we have to do."

He took a deep breath and looked around with cold, dark and steely, eyes. Almost everybody thought he looked directly at them. "I will be honest with you…and I want to tell you a true story," he smirked a slimy smile and immediately began to spill out his tale:

"When I was fighting in the jungle, a colleague was caught in machine gun fire. I could either run the other way or help him. My strong instincts made me take the latter choice and I ran to help the dying man in the grassy clearing. As I approached…," Maxwell paused to take an emotional breath. He looked down towards the ground, feigning tears in his eyes, and then up to the ceiling. "At that moment," he continued, "I saw a giant cobra fall from a tree on to his body." Some editors gasped, as he raised his voice. "A shrill cry came from my friend's mouth, along with the stench of vomit from his gut, as the giant snake lashed out at his helpless prey. My rapid approach made the cobra quickly slither away and I stared for a moment at the distraught body of my colleague—a soldier, a fighter—now on the ground among the green and leafy moulds, with two lethal fang marks on his right arm. The poison from the snake bite would soon spread; I knew that. My military training taught me to act quickly around death. I did no more than rip the scarf from my neck and quickly tied a tourniquet around his arm, then I grabbed the knife from my belt, and without further thought, I hacked off his arm."

We all sat there stunned – not knowing whether to laugh or cry. I thought it was a riveting story but noticed some people were almost asleep, mainly due to lack of air and too much body heat. Did we believe him? Maxwell had started speaking again:

"I saved my friend's life that day, my action was successful, but only because I stopped the poison spreading by cutting off his right arm. He survived."

The moral of the story was certainly sinking in. In the silence that followed, someone coughed; one of the older editors snored. It was just a few seconds, but seemed an age before anyone spoke.

"I will be meeting with your Union Officers soon," said Maxwell. "And, please, wake that man up!" he said pointing to Robin, the wartime history editor. Robin had obviously heard this story before. With that Robert Maxwell turned and left the room; the posse followed sheepishly behind him.

What was to become of us now, we thought?

To be continued….

* * *

Local Retiree Carves a Legacy: Jack Weller aka "Mr. Chips"

John Tabellione

Ask Jack Weller—a thickset, retired, East Cobb manufacturing manager with heavy jowls and massive hands— how he spends his leisure time. He might respond curtly with self-deprecation, saying all he does is sit and "make chips all day." Observe him in his sawdust-coated workshop and you sense immediately that this, seemingly gruff "Mr. Chips" has a soft heart for nature and a surgeon's touch as a wood carver extraordinaire.

Weller's creative expertise is not your grandfather's idea of "whittlin'" away on a tree branch or small block of wood with a pocket knife, trying to fashion an animal figurine. Weller is careful to explain that his avocation represents a whole next generation of carving. Ironically, he did not pick up the trait directly from his dad.

As he tells it, back in his home town of Lancaster, Pennsylvania, the plant manufacturing managers would often take a morning coffee break at a local diner to shoot the breeze, discuss politics and talk shop. One of the guys walked into the group one day, boasting about a wood duck he had carved. Looking at the piece, Weller did not make any critical comments then, but harrumphed to himself: "I can make a duck *whole lot better* than *that*."

That was thirty years ago and "Mr. Chips" hasn't stopped improving upon his first duck and ensuing work. He has taken it several levels higher since winning his first competition in Easton, Maryland at the prestigious Ward Foundation competition, where he won a blue ribbon for a white-fronted goose, only his second creation after the duck. Weller has since tried to discard that original duck several times, but his wife, Marian, religiously hauls the relic out of the trash whenever her husband cleans up his work area.

More recently, in the late nineties, Weller's fame went to the top of the totem pole at the Atlanta Woodworker's Guild exhibition: his amazingly realistic bird carvings took home First, Second and Third place awards from the judges, and he was voted "Best of Show" by the attendees.

Most people would have rested on their laurels, but not this wood maestro: his next phase of carving truly rose another notch. Soon after he encased his prize-winning red-tailed hawk, his songbirds, and other fabulous bird art in Plexiglas displays, he turned to history for further inspiration, saying, while he is still passionate about feeding and observing his real feathered friends, he felt he had mastered making facsimiles of them in wood.

The works of 17th century Dutch-English master woodworker, Grinling Gibbons, is often recognized as the epitome of woodcarving. Weller just might be a reincarnated protégé of Gibbons, having thoroughly studied his biography as well as all of his works. Gibbon's style is described by Weller as flamboyant, with graceful cascades of flowers, fruits, and foliage. Upon reading and studying black-and-white and color lithographs of his art, Weller sets out, again and again, to emulate the intricate work of this peerless carver, because he says he loves classical art with substance.

Dividing a lithograph into quadrants, Weller draws free-hand to copy the elaborate floral, lace-like compositions of the master. Next, he magnifies the art by several sizes on to oak tag paper. Then he proceeds with a 'ponce wheel' to create hundreds of marks or dots on a three-foot long block of basswood, which is only two, or two and a half, inches thick.

While this method of designing sounds neat and simple, it is painstaking and requires the touch and patience of a master. Looking back to his high school aptitude tests, Weller relates, however, that whenever he took such tests, the results always indicated he was artistic.

Still, even he could not visualize himself sitting in front of a canvas using oils, acrylics or pen-and-ink. Little did he foresee that someday his art mode would be three-dimensional and that he would eventually come to use the creative side as well as the analytical/mechanical side of his brain.

An expert carver needs to know exactly how to use the instruments that will bring the required form out of his wood. In Weller's case, his tool collection includes many carving chisels, skews and gouges, rubber mallets, knives, wood burners, and miniature finishing tools, to name a few. In total, he has thousands of dollars invested in tools, but the art he produces with them is priceless. His cabinet drawers contain an assortment of flower and leaf patterns, wax fruit, old photographs, and even a few leftover birds' eyes and feet—plastic versions, that is.

During his interview, Weller absent-mindedly throws on his gun-metal gray, magnifier visor, reminiscent of a welder's mask and a pair of World War II bomber pilot goggles. Instinctively, he grabs a gouge from a tray on a shelf and spots a square edge on a leaf that needs to be rounded—perfected.

He uses basswood, a soft wood recognized as the mainstay of carvers. In fact, Gibbons used the same species, but Europeans call it limewood. The tree from which basswood and limewood originate is the linden tree. It is most appropriate then, that the carved wood of this tree continues to bear fruit and flowers, long after the timber is harvested, through this art. Weller has created dozens of floral and leafy festoons replicating Gibbons' European style. On other occasions he ventures out on his own into new variations and original designs.

Gibbons' signature piece, other than his many invaluable contributions to St. Paul's Cathedral in London, is a cravat he fashioned that was so realistic, it was actually worn on one occasion by the noted English writer and politician, Horace Walpole. Weller reproduced a stunning likeness of the multi-pleated bow and knotted piece, and has gone two articles of clothing better. A denim work shirt, once sitting on a nearby hanger, is now a wooden replica, complete with folds and creases. It hangs on the wall in his study, coated with shellac, which gives it a startling real, starched and ready-to-wear appearance. Weller also duplicated a wooden pair of work shoes, complete with laces and wrinkles that will floor any visitor, every time.

Weller rarely ever paints any of his subjects because, as he puts it, you "never know what's under that paint." He would rather be a purist than cover up blemishes by painting. Another of his idiosyncrasies is that, while he uses some finishing bits and wood burning tools to feather the birds, he does not succumb to power tools to extract the tens of thousands of chips he has made.

As you might imagine, when 'Mr. Chips' creates, it is not work or a task to him; it is done for the sheer love and pleasure of art. Time spent per piece is never recorded. Time is "meaningless" he says when he is concentrating on a project. When asked to name the opus he most prefers, Weller alludes to the current piece in hand as his favorite.

So what goals has he set for himself lately? He is now on his fifth garland where he utilizes thicker, three-inch stock. The challenge, he explains, lies in carving more deeply with thin pieces of wood. The deeper he goes, the better he is able to get more shadow and stronger relief. The intention is to achieve such results to reflect the floral arrangement more like fine art. It also allows him to expand his imagination, yet it is this "visualization" that is the hardest challenge of all. As a truly gifted artist, however, he eventually comes to know it when he sees it.

Marian Weller will tell you the irony is that the crusty, but loveable, "Mr. Chips" to the outside world, transforms into a perfectionist in the world of his art, where he has an everlasting reservoir of patience to perform the multiple, meticulous removals of miniscule bits of wood. Her husband reasons that he has the ability to be patient because "I love art."

(Over the course of his work career, the late World War II veteran was quite proud of the eighteen patents he owned. More likely, however, it will be his dozens of magnificent creations that will leave a far greater legacy for his family and to the world of art and wood carving.)

Ghost Train

John Sheffield

At breakfast one morning in the 1970s, my wife's stepfather, Victor, announced he needed to get some money from his bank in London, and would take the ten o'clock train into Paddington Station. He had done this trip many times. Back then, the trains were punctual, so he was ready to board when, at about ten, the train arrived.

His compartment had facing bench seats, with three women and two men facing each other. Victor had a quick look at the women. None caught his fancy, so he immediately started to read the book he'd brought with him. Absorbed in his book, he and paid little attention to the other passengers, noting only that another couple got on during a brief stop at Reading Station. The clickety-click of the wheels on the rails had a soporific effect and he began to drop off. Clickety-click, clickety-click…click, click, click…he looked up. The train was switching tracks to the left; maybe the platform would be a different one than before. He looked at his watch, ten fifty-five—odd. Normally the ride took around fifty minutes; they should have reached Paddington by now. Then the train entered a tunnel, and Victor did not remember a tunnel. They remained in darkness for a few minutes. Victor was getting worried.

When they emerged into the light, Victor looked at his fellow passengers. They appeared unconcerned, but Victor was worried.

"This may sound like a silly question," he said, "but where is this train going?"

They all laughed.

"It is a silly question," a woman giggled.

"Why?"

"Because we don't know."

The passengers were now giving Victor their full attention.

"I'm sorry, I don't understand what you mean." Victor was really worried now.

"You're joking," somebody muttered.

"No. Where are we going?"

"We don't know. This is a mystery tour."

Can you imagine the shock? Victor had never heard of such a thing.

"A what?" Victor asked.

"We all paid to take a day trip on this train," a florid-faced man answered. "The fun part is that we don't know where it will take us, except it will be on the coast somewhere."

"I thought we were going to the south coast," a lady in a floral dress said. "But we're going north of London, so I guess it will be the east coast."

"Probably Southend or Ipswich," the man suggested.

Victor was horrified. "They're miles away, and I have to get to my bank before it closes at three. When will we get there?"

"Between twelve-thirty and one, we were told."

"But then I'd have to get a train back. I'll never make it to the bank in time."

"Looks like it," the lady replied sympathetically.

When Victor got home that night, he told me this story. I remember asking him what was going through his mind when the lady said they didn't know where they were going.

"I thought I had died," Victor replied. "I knew the old ticker had given out at last, Jane. I was on the train that takes you to the Pearly Gates and Saint Peter. Or worse, I was in a Fellini film."

"What did you do?" I said.

"Well, shortly after the revelation about the tour, the train stopped at a signal," Victor replied. "I opened the door and got out by the side of the track. The passengers shouted encouragement as I scrambled up the embankment. I soon found out the place was a park in the Golders Green area of north London, a few miles from the City. Nearby was a tube station." Victor grinned. "I made it to the bank in time. Not bad for a septuagenarian."

NOVEL BEGINNINGS

Aftermath **Excerpt**   **George Weinstein**

Different Colors   **Brenda Sevcik**

Aftermath Excerpt

George Weinstein

The following is Chapter 1 of the Southern mystery novel *Aftermath*, to be published in October 2016. Purchase complete, autographed paperback copies or e-book versions of *Aftermath* through the author's website: **GeorgeWeinstein.com**.

Summary

Janet Wright left Graylee, Georgia at five, when her mother fled a destructive marriage. Now forty and reinventing herself after a failed engagement, Janet returns as the sole inheritor of her recently murdered father's valuable estate. Life should be easy, but she can't resist pulling at the threads of the apparently open-and-shut case. Before long, she finds herself tangled in Graylee's web of secrets, lies, and scandals—and in fear of her own life, targeted by a mysterious new killer.

Chapter 1

Only one stop, I promised myself, and then I'd go to my father's house—where he had been murdered in July. I wasn't exactly looking forward to that. On Main Street in tiny Graylee, Georgia, I parked the rental car I'd picked up after landing in Atlanta that morning. Seventy-degree weather in late December and BBQ smoke on the breeze through my open windows reminded me I had returned to the Deep South, way below the Gnat Line.

Though I'd been born in Graylee, I only lived there until I was five and had no memory of it. I assumed the place would be just another backwater burg, decorated as countless others were a few days before Christmas. However, instead of check-cashing parlors and pawnshops, the town somehow supported quaint bistros, boutiques selling luxury goods, and salons for hair, nails, and full-body spa treatments, with upscale cars parked in front of each one. Manhattan it wasn't, but it wasn't the sticks either.

How had they maintained such prosperity in the middle of nowhere? Between that and the weather, the place was a modern Shangri-La. If I were back home in the center of the universe, I would've still needed the heavy coat I'd worn while catching a cab to LaGuardia, and which now covered my purse in the front seat. I pushed it aside so I could retrieve my hairbrush and lipstick. As I touched up, I surveyed Main Street again.

The variety of dining and shopping options surprised me, but the best part was a silence I never experienced except when I got out of New York City. No radios blasting, jackhammers machine-gunning concrete, or car horns blaring. The hush and the temperature put me in the mood for a nap but that meant going to Dad's house. I just didn't want to deal with it yet. Too many conflicting emotions, including a helping of dread as big as the deli counter at Zabar's.

At least the remarkable surroundings made me stop wondering for a moment whether I'd been foolish to quit a good job on Wall Street, leave my friends and everything I loved, and return to a home I no longer remembered. From the looks of it, Graylee seemed like a fine place to start over. To give my life a little meaning. To finally do something that mattered.

After exiting my rental and locking it with the remote, I noted a few elderly shoppers jaywalking across the road to their Beamer. They didn't look like the type to hotwire a car and go joyriding. If I planned to live here, I needed to start blending in. Feeling ridiculous but determined to establish new habits, I unlocked the car. After all, probably the only crime committed in Graylee in the past six months had been my father's murder, and the police shot the guy who'd done that.

The phone in my back pocket had been vibrating periodically with texts from friends who demanded updates on my adventure "down South." A new one buzzed my butt. With nothing significant to report yet, I let the messages accumulate unanswered.

I pushed open the door of a gift shop, and sleigh bells jangled. The Christmas murals on the windows had been painted with skill, drawing me inside, but who could I buy a present for? With my father's death, I had no family left. My New York friends were much too sophisticated to appreciate anything from small-town Georgia. Andy Jessup had broken off our engagement six months ago, and—unheard of for me—I hadn't rebounded with another guy yet. I'd always feared I would be all alone at forty, and here I was.

A housewarming gift, I decided, glancing at the displays of yuletide cheer. For my new home, which I'd never seen. Perfect. I took a breath and settled into browse mode, letting my gaze drift over the aisles of goods as my boots led me up a random row.

"Can I help you find something, honey?" A middle-aged woman, wearing a snowflake sweater despite the warm weather, approached me from the back of the shop.

"Just looking," I said, picking up a plush reindeer and putting it back on the shelf. Did that sound too abrupt? "Thank you," I added, drawing out the vowels to sound less like a damn Yankee than a Southern girl who had gone to live among them when I was young.

The woman asked, "You passing through?" Obviously my twang hadn't fooled her. She wove her way among the displays of reds and greens, putting on half-moon glasses that had dangled from a beaded cord around her neck. "Oh, Ms. Wright," she said, taking me in from across a display of holly boughs and fluffy snowmen, "Um, welcome to Graylee."

Small town living, where everybody knew everybody else's business. Maybe someone had spotted me dawdling in my rental car and sent a warning to all of Graylee that Brady Stapleton's daughter had arrived in town.

"Thanks," I said. "Please call me Janet."

"I'm Paulina Lollybelle O'Shea." Her snowflake-clad arm reached over the shelf, and she shook my hand in a perfunctory way. "I'm sorry for your loss." Her delivery was robotic, chilly.

"I appreciate that," I said, hoping I didn't sound as puzzled by her tone as I felt.

"You take after your mama—right pretty, the spittin' image of Mary Grace."

The folksy compliment surprised me. I patted down the cowlick on the back of my head, a gift handed down from Mom. "You knew her?"

"Yes, ma'am, went through school with her. She was a peach. Never understood what she saw in your daddy, though." Her look suggested I had some explaining to do on my mother's behalf. "They made the strangest couple, with her such a petite beauty and him a big ol' bear of a man, bless his heart."

From photographs I'd found on the Internet, that described him well. I said, "I don't remember my father. In fact, I hadn't seen him, or even talked to him, in thirty-five years."

"I reckoned, what with you having your mama's last name." Her voice dropped then, as if the plastic Santa Clauses could overhear us. "Did she tell you about him?"

"No, she never talked about my dad."

"Well, he just about owned Graylee. We heard you were coming down all the way from New York City to be the new owner." She didn't look pleased by this latest Northern incursion.

I own a town, I reminded myself. It was impossible to wrap my mind around. Paulina's sour expression and the possibility that the people here were already gossiping about my arrival got the better of me. Although I had inherited my mother's looks and I carried her name, the one thing she would say about Dad was that I'd gotten his smart mouth. I snapped, "I promise to be a benevolent dictator."

Paulina's eyebrows rose over the tops of her glasses. Then her look of shock turned to delight, and I realized the depth of my mistake. Soon all of Graylee would hear about my snotty declaration.

Damn. I needed to make friends and allies, not score points. Wincing, I shook my head. "Sorry, bad joke. What I meant to say is I'm not planning on running anything—my father seemed to have put really good people in charge. It's not broken, and I don't want to risk breaking it."

The apology seemed to mollify her, or at least she realized what poor manners she was displaying, too. She re-spaced some holiday tchotchkes on her side of the shelf and changed the subject. "All of us sure are glad about what happened to that Wallace Landry."

I nodded at the name of the drifter who had murdered my father. "I guess everyone was spared a pointless trial."

"And fifty years of that horrible man on Death Row," Paulina added, "filing endless appeals. I know it's not the Christian thing to say, but he got what he deserved." She looked at me hopefully, as if seeking something we had in common, a means of building a bond. Either that, or she was setting a trap to get some more juicy quotes she could broadcast.

I said, "You're right, I guess. Although I would've liked to ask him why he did it."

"Because he was evil, you hear? Came into the shop one time, and I knew the moment I laid eyes on him that he had the devil inside. What he did shook up Graylee something awful. We hadn't had a murder in years."

"He probably made everyone here feel nervous about strangers…but, uh, I hope I fit in and won't be considered an outsider much longer."

"Plan on staying, do you?"

It seemed more like a threat than a question, but I soldiered on. "I thought I'd volunteer, maybe start a charity. And work on a book I've always wanted to write."

"Why, honey, we already have an author: David Stark. Maybe you've heard of him?"

Who hadn't heard of the South's answer to Stephen King? I felt another emotional bruise from the passive-aggressive Q&A, but the woman did succeed in making me want to quit procrastinating and escape to my father's house.

"Sure," I said. "I just want to try it. I'm not going to compete with him or anything."

"He even did a holiday story." She pointed at a tall display of hardback books, green dustcovers ornamented with blood splatters, which she'd arrayed in the conical shape of a Christmas tree. Her expression showed pride in Graylee's favorite son and more than a touch of scorn, as if challenging my right to try to write anything.

So much for Shangri-La. Feeling cornered, I said in my mother's sweet Georgia drawl, "But can't there be more than one writer, even in lil' ol' Graylee?" Then I hammered her with my usual don't-screw-with-me New York accent: "Since I own this freaking town and everything in it."

Including the lease on your shop, I hoped my toothy smile conveyed.

At first I took some satisfaction at how Paulina paled to the color of her ridiculous sweater, but then I felt guilty for lording it over the woman. So this is what it was like to have power. First chance I got I'd wielded it like a club instead of an olive branch.

"Of course, of course," she replied, backing down the aisle, palms out as if to ward off another blow. "Um…you, uh, still need help finding a gift?"

"Actually I'd better go." Although the woman had been beyond rude, I added, "Sorry, I was out of line. I'm a long way from home and feeling like an exposed nerve."

That stopped her retreat. "Think nothing of it, honey. We just got off on the wrong foot is all. I hope you'll come back in, and hello me when we see each other around town."

"Count on it." We exchanged wary goodbyes, and I headed outside, sleigh bells ching-chinging behind me. The shame I felt continued to sting. I'd acted like a bully. "Benevolent dictator" would've been an upgrade.

Grimacing over my shortcomings, I checked the GPS on my phone for the drive to Dad's house and then pressed the remote to unlock the car door before remembering my "when in Rome" resolution. Of course, if Paulina's attitude indicated of how everyone in Graylee felt toward me, I probably needed to lock my doors after all. Hell, I might want someone to do a daily bomb sweep.

As I drove down Main Street, I noted two blinking caution lights at cross streets. Steering with my wrists, I took a photo through the windshield to share with my friends later: Look, there aren't even real stoplights here; three cars going in the same direction would constitute a traffic jam. However, my picture also would show them clean gutters and not a single spray of graffiti on the buildings. There were some nice things about small-town living.

The GPS stated, "Take left onto Brady Stapleton Boulevard." I was starting to get a feel for my father. Not exactly humble. And "Boulevard"—seriously?

Ahead, I spotted a Denny's Restaurant, which seemed out of place with the upscale finery. Beyond it, I turned left onto a narrow strip of blacktop instead of the usual pitted concrete. Thick woods lined both sides. Not only was the ride much smoother, but the sound of the rubber against the road was like high-pitched singing. Dad probably had kept his boulevard tuned, so the angelic choir would stay in proper voice. I wiggled the steering wheel back and forth, serpentining across the single lane, and listened to the heavenly song rise and fall.

My father had located his house on the only spot in town with any real elevation. It was just a steep hill with trees all around it, but I half-expected the GPS to announce, "Arriving at Brady Stapleton Mountain." Nothing was modest about the house, however. The sprawling stone hunting lodge covered most of the hilltop.

In the pea-gravel curve of courtyard that fronted the house, I stopped near an iron lawn jockey. The figure's face and hands had been painted bright white, but chips and scratches revealed black paint underneath. If all of this truly belonged to me, the jockey would be the first thing to go.

The granite manse boasted a deep, wraparound porch and an equally impressive balcony that bordered the entire second floor. No one greeted me. My father's lawyer had specified that, after the holidays, a "licensed, insured, and bonded" cleaning crew could tend the house and landscape each week for me. Perhaps that was in reaction to the drifter, Wallace Landry, who'd talked his way into the job of groundskeeper back in late June and thanked my father a few weeks later with seventeen bullets at pointblank range.

I called the lawyer, Mr. Pearson, who also was the executor of the estate, to let him know I'd arrived. Then I walked up the steps and followed the porch in a counterclockwise trek around the house. Clusters of cushioned outdoor furniture provided small oases on the wide expanse of wood. In back of the house, a flagstone walkway led to a four-car garage of stacked stones and slate roof that was larger than the apartment my older brother, our mother, and I had shared after she'd taken us from Graylee to the Atlanta suburbs. It was impossible not to feel anger at how he had thrived while we struggled.

Dad never once paid a dime of alimony or child support, and he'd played no role in our lives. Because Mom had refused to talk about him—other than assigning blame for my smart mouth—I was confused back in July when the Graylee police chief called with news of his murder. In my mind, Brady Stapleton had been dead for years. My brother and mother were gone as well, and here I was, the sole heir, surveying the prosperity that had been denied us.

The book I wanted to write was about Mom's life, a tribute to her strength and fortitude. I would be writing fiction because she had seldom talked about her past, so I'd pieced together fragments over the years and had to imagine the worst parts, including her marriage to the man who had come to own Graylee. I hoped to learn more about both of them, so I could do her story justice.

At the same time, I wanted to be anywhere else instead of dealing with the aftermath of Dad's violent death. Except maybe back in New York, avoiding all of my favorite places for fear of running into Andy or any of my other former boyfriends. At least I was far from all of them.

Settled in a porch rocker facing the courtyard, I finally answered the accumulated texts with as much positivity as I could muster and was moving on to Facebook when a Cadillac pulled up behind my rental car. Mr. Pearson, no doubt. He checked his wavy white hair in the rearview mirror, emerged from his Caddy, and smoothed his suit jacket. Good-looking guy, mid-sixties, with a trim build and a dedicated golfer's tan.

Out of habit, I clocked his ring finger and saw a thick gold band there. Pity, he was just my type: well-heeled and debonair, a mature gentleman. Not that I had refrained from dating a few unhappily married Baby Boomers in New York—which was how my relationship with Andy had started—but such risky behavior would be much harder to pull off in Graylee. New start, new habits, I reminded myself.

The lawyer called, "First impressions of the homestead, Ms. Wright?"

"It's big even by New York standards." I waited for him to get closer so I didn't have to keep shouting. "Are you sure my dad lived alone? He could've stashed at least four women here, and they never would've seen each other."

Mr. Pearson frowned at me, apparently still not used to my sense of humor despite six months of phone calls about the estate. "Brady only dated one at a time," he said, "for as long as I can remember."

He strode up the porch steps, cordovan wingtips glistening. When he shook my hand, I caught the flash of a chunky gold cufflink and matching watch. The lawyer was even more handsome up close, with Coke-bottle green eyes and a regal posture. I had to remind myself again to behave.

"After your mother left," he said, "Brady threw himself into his work, and then there was no time for marriage. The pressures were enormous—nearly everybody's prosperity in Graylee was tied to decisions he made."

That got my attention. I asked, "Is everyone now counting on me to do the same?"

"Not at all. I did not mean to steer us in that direction." He inquired about my plane trip from New York and my journey by car from Atlanta. The gentleman chatted effortlessly, his Southern manners impeccable. Although his precise diction and refusal to use contractions made me self-conscious about how I sounded, I relaxed into my first non-hostile encounter since arriving.

As the man continued to talk, however, I wondered if he charged by the quarter-hour and was padding his bill to the estate. And now the estate was mine. The image of a taxi meter scrolling out of control motivated me to get on with things. Interrupting him, I said, "Look, I know you're a busy man, and we've got lots to do. How do we get started?"

Mr. Pearson produced a large ring of keys from his pocket. "First allow me to give you the tour." He unlocked the front door, opened it, and stepped back. "After you, Ms. Wright."

Afternoon sunlight bathed the interior, a huge open space with exposed stone and timbers, reinforcing the impression of a hunting lodge. The cool air smelled of recently applied lemon furniture polish, leather, and old cigar smoke. Oversized chairs and couches, upholstered in maroon, navy blue, and deep green, offered plenty of seating in the great room.

Thank God there were no animal heads or taxidermied fish on the walls. Mounted there instead were large color and monochrome photographs of different portions of my dad's domain, each rendered with genuine artistry: the little town of Graylee, a light industrial center, a timber nursery with its own plant and rail yard, and plantation-style pecan groves. He'd hired a shutterbug with a great eye for details and moody lighting. Still, the images were unsettling—as if Dad had wanted to survey his whole kingdom at all times.

The central focus of the room was a gigantic pass-through fireplace, the opening roughly eight feet wide and taller than my five and a half feet. Thinking about the seventy-degree temperature a few days before Christmas, I wondered if a hearth could be useful more than a handful of days each winter. Over the piled, fresh-looking firewood, I could see partway into the other half of the room—a dining area with a table fit for a CEO and seating for about twenty.

As Mr. Pearson led me around and described the tons of stone and lumber and the Herculean efforts that had gone into the construction of the house, I verified the dining room actually sat twenty-four. I imagined the elaborate dinner parties held there while Mom worked two jobs and my brother and I babysat, mowed lawns, and did other after-school work to put a little more food on our secondhand table. It made me wonder for the umpteenth time since I was told of my inheritance why we couldn't have enjoyed at least a little bit of his prosperity. Now I could immerse myself in the whole opulent lifestyle, but had no one to share it with me: a queen in a deserted castle.

A guest bathroom, complete with walk-in shower, and an expansive kitchen took up the rest of the space on that side of the fireplace. The appliances and granite countertops looked pristine, without a smudge or any discoloring from usage. My mother's blender had been held together with duct tape, and our refrigerator had looked like tornado salvage. As for my own belongings, due to arrive after Christmas in a moving van, nothing would go with what I'd seen so far. My stuff was urban shabby chic, not gentlemen's club. How would I fit my life into this house?

"There are east and west guest wings down here," the lawyer said, "as well as two spare bedroom suites upstairs." Near both wings, wood staircases led up to the second floor, where hallway doors opposite the guest wings allowed entrance to the master suite. Mr. Pearson led the way again, resuming his tour-guide patter. The master had the same dimensions as the huge room beneath us, with the stone chimney bisecting it. We stood in a study with bookshelves crammed full of hardcovers and paperbacks—including all of David Stark's titles—a table-size TV with a manly leather recliner and a matching couch, and a computer desk that had a southern exposure, looking down on my father's "boulevard" and the town beyond it.

Mr. Pearson said, "The other side, Ms. Wright, is…well, um, I will give you a little privacy." He stepped into the hall and closed the door behind him.

I eyed the stonework of the chimney and imagined Dad's bedroom on the other side of it. No doubt the furnishings would be über-masculine. On a moonless night in July, with Dad asleep there in blue silk pajamas, Wallace Landry had inched open the door from the hallway, stepped softly over the rugs and heart-pine planks, and shot my father to pieces.

From local newspaper articles and TV reports I'd found online, I knew Landry had been twenty-six years old and roamed from town to town doing odd jobs. A big, fair-haired guy, handsome in a scruffy way, with a careless kind of smile. Probably a real charmer, in addition to being a homicidal maniac. I pictured how the gunfire would have lit up the dark room and revealed Landry in brief, intense flashes, the sounds echoing around the enormous space like the end of the world.

Maybe Dad had flaunted his status in a town that depended on him for jobs. Maybe he had been a monster to Mom and totally uncaring about my brother and me. Maybe I'd even fantasized over the years about what it would've been like to find him alive and punish him for the ways he'd wronged us. If nothing else, I wished I'd had the chance to confront him before Landry pulled the trigger.

Likewise, I would've liked to ask the drifter why he had done it before he was gunned down in the same room. The police chief had not arrived fast enough to stop the crime, but at least he had executed the criminal.

I wanted to continue dawdling, even if it meant torturing myself with further gruesome imaginings, but Mr. Pearson waited on the other side of the door. Rounding the chimney, I walked upon the murder scene.

Purchase autographed paperback copies or e-book versions of *Aftermath* through the author's website: **GeorgeWeinstein.com**.

Different Colors
Brenda Sevcik
<u>Chapter One</u>
Pain
Celine

Pain has a memory. It has color and texture and remembers exactly where it left you. If it leaves inhaling, when it returns days, weeks, months later, it returns in full force exhaling. I know because I have breathed this memory many times. That's why when pain resurrects itself, I avoid, I hide, and if necessary, I medicate. I do everything I can to leave this misery breathless, and send it back to the tomb.

I'm a nurse and understand. I used to look at my patients' faces and try to assess how pain had invaded them. I would observe the creases between their eyebrows, the tension in their mouths, the rhythm of their breath, and the tightness of their hands. I would look and ask them to give me a number for their discomfort, guessing it before they spoke. Their number was always close, but usually underrated. Most people so desperately wish to deny their own suffering.

The problem was their pain became *my pain*. My memory latched right onto their real misery, and ripped right down into my gut. I would hyperventilate, clench my teeth, and need to squeeze something. Remaining calm, I would look at their charts and see what kind of relief medication they were allowed, maxing out whatever the doctor prescribed; I could not allow this pain to deepen its memory.

Now I simply go into my patient's room and ask how they are feeling, avoiding all eye contact. Grabbing the chart and carefully reviewing all the meds, I do their vitals, ask their discomfort intensity number, and do what needs to be done to deaden their pain. My patients are well cared for and the agony is crucified, if possible.

My superior has said my patients think me unfriendly. They say I never smile, make small talk or make them feel like they are a real person by looking at them in the eye. I just can't anymore. I simply *feel others pain too deeply.* It is impossible to explain. I've tried.

Still I have no doubt I'm a good nurse. I have had to let go of my ego and realize my patients may not understand that I am a soldier fighting for them. In the future, when pain returns for them, it won't be as bad, as I've stopped their memory from advancing. Because of my expertise, in the end they *are* better off, whether or not they give me credit. I know what I know, and I fight this battle for my patients.

I have decided my war by osmosis has a reason, and my patients' benefit.

****

Tonight I am home, not working. I have made a healthy cabbage and navy bean soup, with whole wheat bread that has a fresh nutty taste, and the real butter makes me think of dessert as I eat it. Mia and Mack in turn protest the contents of this meal, but I insist they try. They decide it's fine. The warm broth fills their tummies with love and comfort and they laugh and tease and we are all happy. They insist on raspberry jam on top of the buttered bread, and pretending to protest, I give it to them anyway. We clean up and it's time to get ready for bed.

They bathe, brush their teeth and we sing silly songs that make no sense. We decide on Mack's bed tonight. He chooses a simple book and we decide to cuddle up with Mia reading. She is proud of her skills, and I allow her every chance to practice. Mia's words sound like music to me, and I allow each word to dribble down my cerebral cortex and spine, then circle my belly. There is nothing better. If pain has a memory, color and texture, joy does too. It's warm and violet and smooth and I wrap my heart around it.

Abruptly the door to the bedroom opens. The children remain oblivious to their dad entering, deep into the best climactic part of the story. I am aware. Turning my head I lock eyes with Abbott for a moment, but must quickly look away. The joy spell has been shattered, I feel his jagged edges—and all warmth has been replaced with my husband's cold anguish. He hurts. Pain is occupying him, and I feel what he feels.

Mia sees him. "Hi, Daddy! I'm reading to Mack! Come listen!" Mia is proud, but both children are so drawn into the story, they quickly return their focus to the book. Neither notices Abbott has shut the door without a word. I listen and hear his steps into the kitchen. The soup pot's lid is raised and loudly dropped. The refrigerator door opens, then is slammed shut. Maybe he remembers he forgot to give me grocery money, and I had to do with what little I had. But no, his steps thunder from the kitchen to the garage, and he is angry. The outside door opens and closes. He has left.

The residue of his pain has remained. I hold my breath. I cannot try to polish the rough fringes around the perimeter of his heart, fill his lungs with life, or be a soldier and fight for him if he's gone. And I cannot exhale until he returns.

Soon the children are sleeping. Mia has passed out in Mack's bed, but it's okay. I see her resting face and am reminded of the intensity chart I give my patients as they evaluate themselves. I assess Mia for her contentment and give the highest marks. She's completely secure and pleased with her day's accomplishments. I leave her there, snuggled next to her little brother.

I am not content. I worry about my husband and ponder why he is so agitated, wondering where he went and when he will be back. I pray pain will not permanently damage him.

Although it is bedtime, I know I will not sleep until Abbott returns. Drawing a lavender bath, I undress and timidly dip my toes in the water, hoping the temperature is just right. I don't want it too hot or too cold. When I'm sure the water is comfortable, I sink my entire body into my tub, desiring relief, wishing I could transfer from Mia and Mack their perfect warmth and contentment. If I could will him the glow of their joy, revive him with a living breath, I would.

Perhaps then my pain would go away too.

Chapter Two

Different Colors

Mia

I wonder when I realized my family was different.

Maybe it was the first time I went to preschool and noticed how the other moms would wait in the hall to pick us up at the end of our day. Like now, Mommy worked nights as a nurse, and mostly slept during the day. But she was always awake enough to pick me up at school. Closest to the door, she was the first mommy we all saw when the teacher opened up the room so we could go home. But Mommy was by herself. Even if she was standing near other mommies, she was alone.

As we walked out, I could see how the other mommies, together, would be chatting outside our classroom door, smiling, sharing stories and laughing like they were in special teams, playing a secret game. If they had teams, they never picked my mommy.

Later in the parking lot the other mom's would wave their hands, with their nails all painted pretty and yell, "Have a great day!" They would nod big smiles, and act like they were best friends. My mommy didn't notice she wasn't included, but I did.

I thought maybe she didn't wave to the other mommies because her fingernails didn't have colors on them. Or maybe they had picked teams, but she wasn't there on that day. Mommy simply wasn't one of them, and I decided that's the way she wanted it. I was okay with it if she was. And I'm still fine with it. She's still different. And it makes our entire family different, too.

I try to name the first time when I realized we were *the other*. Was it when I saw how other families worked, like on the TV, or noticed my neighbors, or hung out with my cousin's family? Or maybe before I was even born. Thinking back on it, I bet I've always felt I was surrounded by *That Which is Different*, maybe even when I was in my mom's belly.

I am not different.

I love art. It's fun to make things that are in my imagination into real, like putting it on paper. Mixing colors with my paints is fun, and I've learned, that if you mix too many colors together you get brown, which is a dark color. Brown is not my favorite, so I don't do that anymore. I've figured that one out quick! It's best when I'm with someone else, especially Mommy. I love it so much when she sits at the table with me and makes art. She's not as good as me, and asks how she should do things. "How do I get green?" She raises her voice like a question mark. She listens very carefully to me when I tell her. She usually does okay after that, but mostly it's just fun to have her sit down and have her attention. Especially when my brother, Mack, isn't around because he's four and makes what mommy calls chaos.

I'm good at sports, too. When we play kickball in my second grade class, I'm always the first one to get picked for the team. Before I even kick the ball, I can see in my head exactly how to kick it, and when I do, it goes right where I want it to go. Mommy says it's one of my special gifts. I guess the other kids in my class know it, too.

I have lots of friends in school. Riley is my best friend and at lunch and we sometimes share food. I even trade telephone numbers with her and other kids at school, only I never invite anyone over to play. I figured that out a long time ago, way back in my preschool days.

So far it's been okay. When there's no one around, Mommy concentrates her everything on me. She taught me to read and tie my shoes when I was four, how to play tennis and hit a softball, how to scream so Daddy will kill the spider in my bathroom, and how to microwave frozen dinners. She always hugs me and tells me how special and loved I am. I know she's not lying. I can see it in her eyes, and feel it with her great bear hugs. I love Mommy so much. And she loves me back big time.

I worry about her sometimes. She'll cry at night sometimes after she talks to Grandma or Aunt Scarlett on the phone. Or she'll sit on the computer, looking hypnotized. The blue-grey glow from the screen and her focused eyes would make her look scary, if you didn't know her like I do. When she's dark and locked to her computer she doesn't even say hello when Daddy comes home. On those days she doesn't fix him dinner--not even EasyMac. I know that bothers him. I figured out when she's like that he starts working late or when he does come home, he quickly leaves again to 'go to a meeting'. I think he even goes to work early in the morning before Mommy gets up then comes home after she's asleep when she gets in these dark-colored moods. I guess that way he doesn't have to feel so bad when she ignores him.

I don't know why she ignores him when she's dark. Maybe it's so they don't argue. When she's dark, they fight a lot. They squabble about Daddy not giving her enough money for the groceries, or why Mommy doesn't have a decent meal for him when he gets home, or why he doesn't fix the toilet in the hall that always runs after you flush it. I wish Daddy would notice these moods like I do and just ignore her back so there's not all that noisy yelling when she's dark, but I guess it's real hard for him, too.

When she's dark Mommy hardly ever looks at Daddy. These moods take away her hugs and kisses, and our entire family is flat, like a can of soda left out too long. I guess when you think about it, ignoring each other during her moods would be better and a whole lot more quiet. I feel real, real bad for both of them, but especially bad for Mommy.

So when I'm worried about her, I sometimes color a picture. I think of how the other kids would color a picture of their mom. They would use the basic primary colors: red, yellow, and blue. Not me. I use the different colors from my two hundred and sixty-four pack. Colors like magenta and plum, azure and maize. Colors no one else would use to describe their mom. No one else has a mommy like mine. She is special, and one of a kind, and she has the different colors to prove it.

And I love her.

Chapter Three

When Silence Becomes too Loud

Abbott

Right now if I were Mia, I take my box of crayons, break every one in half and throw them against the fucking pavement. I'd hope the sun would melt them, causing them to be utterly useless. Not only to me. To any goddam son of a bitch who thought they could make something beautiful out of those useless pieces of wax.

I'm getting into my car after a shitty day at work. It would have been better if I had stayed in bed and never gotten up. I feel as if I've been t-boned from the side. I didn't see this one coming.

God. I want a drink so bad. I want a drink so goddamn bad. I can think about is how warm and sweet a double would taste. As I close my eyes, my mouth waters. I lean back into my car seat, visualizing the glass on my lips, and almost feel the burn going down into my gut, spreading heat into my abdomen, tingling to the ends of my fingers and toes. How I want that slurry-relief feeling. Like the tension rope has snapped in two. Damn. Everything would be better if I had a drink, just one—right now.

My boss is an ass and a young son of a bitch. I just know he's going to fuck me out of my commission on the Bryant account. I've nurtured and babied that relationship for months. It was me, not him and his Ivy League MBA that got those assholes at Bryant to even listen to our product. I know my baby-face boss knows *that I'm the one that deserves* every penny for that sale. Why is he trying to finagle himself into the deal?

I don't want to go home. What the hell will I find there? What will Celine have for dinner? Will the kids even care I'm there as they're freewheeling around the house like wild animals, whooping and hollering? Making nothing but noise. Who would want to go home to that?

Where I want to go is the off-sale. Get a pint, put it into my suit coat pocket and go for a walk on the greenway. There I would open up my jacket, pull out my bottle, and take a gulp when no one else is looking. Stress going out, a buzz coming in. Damn! Wouldn't that be perfect? Don't I deserve it?

Still weighing my options with closed eyes in my car, I think. Choices. My choices. My Choice.

Turning the key in the ignition, I fire up my Chevy and decide to go home. I know once I unwind I will be hungry. I try to turn my thoughts to food. Pasta. Chinese. A good fried catfish.

Yeah, fried catfish, hush puppies and cole slaw. Wouldn't a cold beer just wrap up the meal? Guess a guy can dream.

***

Pulling into the garage all I see is a filthy, cluttered mess: Mack's tricycle, Mia's Barbie bike, helmets, tennis rackets, a red gasoline tank, empty, waiting to be filled so I can finish mowing the lawn, paint cans reminding me of unfinished projects. I absorb the obligations, chores, and the fucking crap I need to do and have no desire for. I want to be hungry, but I'm not. I still want that goddamned drink.

Walking into the house, there is an aroma of food, welcoming comfort food. I hear voices inside Mack's bedroom upstairs. There's laughter, happiness and life. Will I be welcomed? Will they let me in? I own the goddamn house. I deserve it!

Standing outside Mack's door, I listen and hear Mia reading. Celine is asking questions, to see if both of them understand the story. I can pick up Mack's impatience as he begs Mia to continue to see what's next. Mia carry's on, her voice steady and complete. I wonder what that feels like: contentment and self-satisfaction and feeling whole. What did it feel like before I had been dealt this fucking stacked deck of cards against me with this new boss and his wily0 ways? What did I do to deserve him?

Entering the bedroom, they don't even know I'm there. I don't matter one goddamned bit. Celine looks up, gives me that fucking wounded look and turns back to the book. Mia finally glances up, says something, but I'm too pissed to process it. I close the door. They won't even miss me. I'm obsolete at this point.

Going into the kitchen I see a loaf of that health-nut crap Celine calls bread she makes from some machine that reminds me of R2D2 from the Star Wars movies. I open the soup pot, and see vegetables without one piece of meat, not even a soup bone. I deserve better; I deserve a real meal. I drop the lid and head back to my car. I'm making my escape, but I don't know where I'm running to.

      I know what I'm supposed to do when I feel like this. I should call Jerry, or Dan, or even Kimberly. But I don't want them to see me in such a shit-ass mess. I feel like one of Mia's discarded Ken dolls I've seen lying around in the corners of her room; limbs all contorted and messed up, all vulnerable, still with that goddamn plastic smile on its lips. I don't have the energy to smile and cover up how I feel with my normal group. It's just not there for me tonight. So I look on my phone and Google a late AA meeting. Somewhere where no one will know me, where no one will expect me to have all my shit together. Somewhere I can just say the words, "My name is Abbott, and I'm an alcoholic. And right now I want a drink so fucking bad."

      As luck would have it, my car is nearly out of gas, so I stop to fill up, spilling some on my hands. I go into the restroom to wash up and see the cigarette ads. Then I remember this meeting allows smoking. I smile to myself and tell myself I deserve it. Although it's been months since my last cigarette, I go inside to buy a pack. If I can't have a drink, I can at least have some smokes. I decide on some weird-ass lady brand, so not to totally get into the habit. When I open up my wallet, I see several twenties in there. On the spur of the moment, I ask for some scratch off tickets, twenty dollars' worth. I deserve the thrill to see if there's a winning ticket under the silver-grey layer of chalky paint. Why not?

      Going outside I light the cigarette, it's thinner and longer than my usual brand and I regret the choice. I pull out a quarter and begin rubbing my scratch-offs. Bingo! I win twenty bucks. I go back in to claim my prize, put in another twenty dollars and buy some more. I keep winning little bits, going back and forth, buying more scratch offs, and before I know it, I've gone through all the money in my wallet, with no winnings to show for it. I glance at my watch. The meeting is probably over, but it's okay; I didn't drink. I retained my sobriety. I got some smokes, and spent some money, but I'm still sober. I didn't blow that.

Then I remember. The money in my wallet was for Celine to buy groceries. I forgot to give it to her this morning. We decided her paycheck would go one hundred percent to get all our credit card and her student loans paid off, and in two years we'd be debt-free. We had decided together on adhering to a tight budget. She told me last night she had nothing to make dinner with, nothing worth eating anyway, and she had no cash. Fuck! What would I give her now?

I feel like my body and mind have been put through a meat grinder. All I want to do is to go home and surrender to sleep and end this shit-ass day. Say goodnight to this disaster, hoping tomorrow will be better.

When I get home I notice there's a bowl of soup on the counter. A generously buttered piece of thick bread is near it, along with a note telling me there's a glass of Hersey's chocolate milk waiting for me. Celine must have just gone to bed; the soup is plenty warm. It's then I realize how hungry I am. I devour the soup, inhale the bread and gulp down the chocolate milk. She's made it rich and dark; just the way I like it. I don't deserve this.

Thinking of Celine, I don't want to go into our bedroom and face her if she's still awake. I spent our grocery money, I left without telling her where I was going, and I smell like sweat, gasoline and cigarettes.

I remember a few nights ago when Mia got her paint on the carpet. She came to me, grabbed my wrist and walked me over to the rug, silent, yet pointing to all these amazing colors she had mixed, but spilled on the floor. Looking down, she was ashamed because she knew better; she knew painting was not allowed in the living room. She expected I would explode in a fury, and I did.

I feel like Mia did that night, and I know I should confess to Celine, but I am afraid to show her the colors of my mess up tonight. I do not want to see her disappointment, bring darkness to her, or feel her anger I know I deserve.

But I know I must walk up those steps. I understand how important it is for me to open our bedroom door, brush my teeth then crawl into bed next to her. If I don't, if I sleep in the guest room like I want to, it will not only seal my guilt, it will send Celine into a worried frenzy.

When I open the bedroom door, the room is cool and smells sweet. Celine remains quiet, and I will her to be asleep. Tip-toeing into the bathroom, I change my clothes and brush my teeth. It's humid in here, and I can tell she's taken a lavender bath for relaxation. I go to the candles surrounding our tub; they are still warm. She hasn't been in bed long. I feel as if my transgressions are written on my forehead in bold, red letters. My body feels heavy, like my limbs are cast in cement.

I take plenty of time to brush my teeth. I decide to shower, hoping with the removal of the smoke and gasoline residue from my hands and hair my guilt will be released. I turn on the shower good and hot then linger, letting the scorching water pound on my flesh, turning it a bright pink. I desire cleanliness, but that feeling doesn't come.

My delays are no longer reasonable. I stop the shower, dress, walk into the bedroom and very quietly lie down next to her.

I can smell the natural healing oils she has slathered on her body after her bath. They remind me of the sacramental oils they used when I was an altar boy. She murmurs my name, pressing her back to me, ready for our spooning position. Her skin is bare and warm and her perfume intoxicating. She invites me in. And as I plunge into her, and feel her very soul vibrate and join mine, I feel anointed and forgiven.

And I know I don't deserve that.

Chapter Four

No more Noise

Mack

We are reading a silly book that doesn't make sense. It says boys are made of snips and snails and puppy dog tails. I look at Mommy and say I'm a little boy, and that's not me. I'm made up of skin and bones, and other things like a brain and a heart. Mommy explains to me that these words are not real things, only that they are meant to put a picture in our brains about what a little boy might be like. She says a snip is someone small, and a snail is slow, the way I am sometimes when she calls and I'm supposed to come so we can pick up Mia at the bus stop. And you know how our dog, Meacham, wags his tail like crazy when we all get home? Could that be how I act when I'm happy? Could these pictures describe me? She stops talking, letting me think. I'm trying to get it, then Mia puts her arm around me and says I'm not made up of those things; I'm made up of noise. Mack you're just lots of noise!

She's laughing and hugging me, so this is a joke. I know I'm not made up of noise. I get what that is. It's when the TV is too loud, or when the fans scream at a baseball game. It's also those times when mostly Daddy talks real loud and fast to Mommy and Mia takes me into my room and helps me get my Lego's out, or she reads me a book. That hasn't happened in a while. That noise in our house has stopped.

The last time there was noise was when Mommy was in one of her closed-door moods, where it's like her smiles are hidden in a shut closet, and her words are mostly asleep. Those are my words to make a picture. Daddy doesn't like it when Mommy is like this, and this day he got loud. Maybe he thought he could scream her out of her mood. When he couldn't, he went outside on the back deck after slamming a real-live door. Now that made some noise!

I went outside to hug Daddy, only he wasn't in a hugging mood. He was looking at the big tree in the yard, but I think he doesn't see it. I told him we need to love Mommy up when she's shut, just like Mommy tells us to love him up when he gets loud.

He turned his head to me. "She tells you what?"

I was afraid my words didn't make sense, but I try real hard. "You know when you're all wiggly and have lots of frowns and talk loud and slam doors like just now? Mommy says it's your way of saying you need love, so we need to smoother you with it." I stop and think of how to make pictures with my words. "You know smoother, like pouring all kinds of Hershey's syrup on ice cream, so you can't even see it because it's covered in chocolate!"

At first I think my words must have made a good picture, because he hugged me, but then he started to cry, and I think maybe I was being silly again.

I don't know how long ago that was really, but it seems like it was far away.

***

Lately Mommy's been teaching me about all kinds of shapes like circles, squares and things with three sides called triangles. I trace a large one with my purple crayon. At the top of this pyramid I draw a picture of Mommy, and then on the bottom Daddy and Mia. Next I put me, Mack, smack in the middle of the triangle. On all our faces are big smiles, and there is no more noise.

PERSONAL MATTERS-2

Good Mothers	Susan McBreairty
Life and Coffee Grinds	Megan Benoit Ratcliff
I've Lost My Mother	Terry Segal
Celebration Conflagration	John Sheffield
Fired	Terry Segal

Good Mothers

Susan McBreairty

Macy McGuire walked down the country road toward her home under a cloudless sky and the light of a full moon. Her fingers and toes felt frozen. It would be painful thawing out.

The moonlight divided the snow covered fields and forest into shades of black and white. Blades of tall grass cast minute shadows that swayed to the chilling wind.

Macy often played too long at her cousins' house and today was no different. She wasn't far from home and didn't need permission to get off the bus there. Many of the townspeople were from the same clan.

They'd built snow forts and had a snowball fight. Macy threw hers with some force and when it made contact, her cousin called out, "That hurt, Macy. Don't throw so hard."

'I might be getting too old for this kid's stuff,' she thought. 'I'm thirteen, after all.' Bringing hands to mouth, she breathed on them but the mittens prevented her hands from absorbing the warmth.

Her gait slowed as she looked toward home. No lights on. Not even the one outside at the front door. Her older brother must not be expected. He came and went with the seasons. But sometimes he'd show up unexpected in the dead of winter. Nor was her father home. He worked away for months at a time. No one thought to tell the children when he'd be coming back or when he was leaving. It seemed the men just came and went.

Looking at the dark house she thought her mother was probably already asleep. Her little sister Joyce was likely at home. Maybe she was hugging a portable transistor radio and listening to the Top 40 hits out of Boston on WRKO-AM, 680. That was one of the best things about winter nights in northern Maine. The radio signal was not strong in the summer or during the day. Just late in wintertime. Wolfman Jack. Casey Casem. The latest and greatest from the outside world.

Macy turned her gaze to her aunt and uncle's house. She longed to be inside. She adored her aunt's lady-like manners, though her aunt's husband never felt like an uncle. He was her Aunt Jackie's second husband and he came from down-country or from out of state maybe. Macy was too young to remember her first uncle before he died in a logging accident. Mr. Nash—he was not known to Macy on a first-name basis—seemed much too tall and gangly to truly fit in with the Scotch-Irishmen of her hometown. Her kinsmen only seemed tall because they had big personalities. They handled powerful machines to cut timber, drove logging trucks, and worked in extreme conditions throughout the year. Mr. Nash also seemed educated.

Macy had begun to feel that men had life so much better than women. She could tell her mother suffered. And she didn't know what she should or could do about it. How can you help someone who doesn't like you? Who doesn't seem to want to hear the sound of your voice? Sometimes Macy experienced self-pity when thoughts of their relationship flooded her mind and heart. It was probably just her imagination that her mother didn't like her. And Macy's imagination was known to get away with her.

Like when she walked across the long one-lane bridge and looked to the tree tops lining the mountain behind her house. Macy pretended the tall trees were castle towers and an amazing life could be lived up there. And not just on top of the mountain; for sure on the other side there were more castles.

It was a Wednesday night and Macy knew from the cars parked outside women had gathered for their weekly Bible study. She wanted to be in their company. Her mother was emotionally erratic and there was never any predicting what kind of mood she'd be in. Countless times she'd heard her mother say, "I wish to God I'd never been born." Or, "My head is coming off. My head is coming off." Worrisome words.

All Macy could do was to pray for her mother. Praying gave her a sense of taking action. She'd begun to grow impatient, though. It didn't seem her prayers were heard.

Inside her aunt's house it would be warm and pretty. On the dining room table, little cakes and pastries nestled beside a choice of coffee and tea.

A soft white glow fell onto the snow outside from behind the lace curtains in the living room windows. Four cars were parked in the drive way. She kept her gaze on the house and surveyed it. Her aunt's house was bigger than the one she lived in. Like her home, it was a two-story with a basement. Downstairs, it had a kitchen, separate dining room, and a living room. What it had that her home did not have was a small foyer and a staircase with a railing. Her house had a stairway up to the bathroom and bedrooms, but there was not a railing. Her father built things but never quite finished them.

Each time she'd been in her Aunt Jackie's house a peaceful feeling enveloped her. Unlike at home. She wanted to burst into the Bible study and yell, "It's not safe for me to go home. May I be here with you?" But she knew better not to betray her mother and father and the whole family for that matter. Macy needed to protect her mother from the worry of what people would say.

Macy loved her mother. That's what you're supposed to do. Honor thy mother and thy father. Because they love you more was the flip side of the commandment. But not all parents can love their children. And yet the Bible also teaches, 'Blessed are the poor and the poor in spirit' for they will see paradise. Or something to that effect. Macy felt poor in spirit.

'I'm going to do it,' she said to herself. 'I'm going in there and I'm going to ask if I can be a part of their gathering.'

She approached the front door and felt her courage begin to drain out of her. 'Not the front door. Go 'round back and go in that way.'

Crouching down and sneaking to the side of the house where the addition had been built for the large kitchen, Macy peeked in the door window and saw Mr. Nash sitting at the kitchen table eating a piece of cake and having a cup of tea. 'Drat,' she thought, 'How will I get passed him?' Macy looked back toward the road but held onto her determination. 'Maybe I don't have to try to get passed him. I could just knock on the door and he'd let me in.'

That's what happened. She knocked and he opened the door. "Why, little Macy, is that you," he asked smiling. She was surprised by his gentle voice and kind face. And just as surprised that he knew her name.

"It is me," she answered. "May I come in? I'm very cold."

"Yes, of course, child. Come right on in. Your mother and sister are here, too."

Macy stopped in her tracks. What? Her mother and sister were there. How and why was that?

"My m-m-mother and sister are here? Why? Why are they here?" she gushed.

"Well, dear Macy, the ladies who meet here weekly have been worried about your mother, and you, and your sister. They decided it was time to reach out to her and invite her here tonight."

"How do you know so much about it," she blurted out and instantly realized how rude that must have sounded.

"I'm pretty sure you're old enough for some straight talk. And I think it's best you hear it from your mother than from me. Though rest assured, I care very deeply for you and your family, as we all do. Wait here a minute," he said.

Macy took off the mittens and breathed into her cupped hands. She felt her fingers begin to throb and knew her toes would start to thaw soon as normal circulation commenced. She wiggled her toes in the boots and stomped them a couple times on the rug by the door to shake off the melting snow. Deliberately lifting one foot and then the other, she set the boots by the door.

Macy felt utter bewilderment. How many invitations had her mother declined that these ladies had extended to her over the years? How often had Macy wished her mother would join in and socialize with the other women? All their neighbors were her father's people. Families her mother had married into and left her parents and family on the other side of the river. This side of the river seemed to remain a foreign land. Her mother stayed isolated and secretive. Macy could not understand why.

The separation of families and cultures the river provided ran dark and deep. As the St. John River flowed east, it cut through forests logged many times over. It had served as a swift thoroughfare for the spring run of timber not so many years ago. Men like her father would skip and hop across the logs when they jammed up. He'd use a peavey to loosen the logs and then scamper back to shore when the logs began to move again. Ultimately, the river becomes the international border between the U.S. and Canada and meets its end in St. John, New Brunswick as it's gobbled up by the Bay of Fundy.

Scotch-Irish Presbyterians, Irish Catholics, and bilingual French-English speaking people comprised the cultural mix in small towns up and down the river. Prejudices abounded among them all. Macy often heard expressions of superiority from her kin. Things said like, "All Catholics are going to hell. The French are stupid and need to speak proper English." She also heard it said about her people that "the Irish are all drunkards and hillbillies."

There also seemed to be a fair share of suicides in Macy's small town; mostly women. She remembered one morning before school, how upset her mother had been and delivered the news that a woman in town had been found hanging from the rafters in the barn behind her home. So dreadful. And another time, a woman took a gun and went to the river bank and shot herself. But it hadn't killed her. She was admitted to a hospital for the mentally ill. She checked herself out of the hospital, walked to a nearby river and out onto the ice until she found a break in it and deliberately fell in. Her body was retrieved down river in the spring.

Macy figured she knew all the women who'd gathered at Aunt Jackie's this evening. She wondered what was taking so long for her to be beckoned into the next room with everyone. She decided to peak around the corner into the dining room. She could see through to the living room.

Sitting in the middle of the living room was her mother. She was surrounded by the women. They were on their knees. Each had laid a hand on her mother. Their heads were bowed and her Aunt Jackie was praying. Macy couldn't make out what was being prayed but the up and down tone of her Aunt's voice assured Macy that earnest words were being spoken.

She couldn't take her eyes off her mother. Her face appeared serene and there was a hint of a smile. She kept her eyes closed as the women prayed over her.

Where was Mr. Nash? Where was her sister, Joyce?

Macy backed up and into the kitchen. She moved to the hallway that led to the front door and tiptoed toward it. The hallway opened to the living room on the right and the stairway was on the left. Approaching the end of the stairway, she saw Joyce sitting on a step peering through the railing into the living room. Multiple voices could now be heard as the group of women continued to pray for their mother.

Joyce raised her index finger to her lips in a gesture to remain quiet and Macy nodded. All they could really do was wait.

Macy was dying to know how all this had come about.

Thinking to herself she wanted to find Mr. Nash, Macy decided to search for his study. She signaled to Joyce, pointing straight up meaning for them to go up the stairs. Something told her that he had the answers.

At first, Joyce shook her head, No. Macy decided it didn't matter if Joyce followed her or not, she was going to seek Mr. Nash out and ask him what was going on.

She hadn't reached the top of the stairs before hearing Joyce coming up behind her. The door to Mr. Nash's study was open and the light was on. Macy and Joyce stepped into the room. Mr. Nash's back was to them and he was bent forward holding a piece of paper. Macy cleared her throat and he turned to face them. His expression was full of thought. Macy could tell that he would be choosing his words very carefully.

He seemed to wake from his contemplations, motioning them to sit on the settee beside his desk.

"I apologize for not returning to the kitchen where you were waiting, Macy. I thought it was best to prepare answers to questions you must have about all this."

In a quiet, serious voice she said, "I understand. Please, what can you tell me?"

"Your mother suffers from an ailment that is very hard to cure. In fact, there is no known cure. It has to do with the way her mind works. Her mind does not help her see how to manage and cope with all the challenges she faces. What is happening here this evening is an attempt to reach your mother's heart and soul. To connect in such a way that she will come to trust the caring community that surrounds her. It's always been here for her but she has not accepted the compassion people have for her."

Joyce began a soft, barely audible sob. Her chin quivered and she sniffled. Mr. Nash handed her a tissue and patted her head.

"It's all right," he said. "Tears will help cleanse the hurt and confusion you've had. I'll bet you've been feeling that way for a long time."

Over the course of the next hour, this kind and gracious man spoke to Macy and her sister with the utmost sincerity and clarity. He said that their mom was going to get the help she needed and the ladies' Bible group was going to see to it.

"Can you force help onto someone?" Macy wondered aloud. "They've offered so many times over the years. Why now? Why do you think it will make any difference now?"

It was Joyce who delivered the simplest truth, "Because you've been praying for her, Macy. Your prayers are being answered."

Could that be true? A brilliant light filled the room. Macy looked at Mr. Nash and Joyce. They did not appear to see the light as she did because there was no wonderment on their faces.

A still small voice said to Macy through the light, "Believe my child. Your prayers have been answered." The light faded leaving Macy with a sense of deep inner peace and sight into the future.

Many hardships lay ahead but the good would outweigh the bad. She was certain of it.

Life and Coffee Grinds
Megan Benoit Ratcliff

I measure out my life in coffee grinds
and empty coffee cups,
as much a natural rhythm of my life
as dawn and dusk,
or the ebb and flow of my faith
over the course of a year,
present but varying in intensity,
sometimes a dark espresso,
sometimes a watered down Folgers.

I've Lost My Mother

Terry Segal

I've lost my mother.

When I was a child that used to mean that I had been separated from her in the grocery store. In the back of Food Fair, by the meat counter, a vending machine magically dropped bottles of NEHI grape or orange soda down a chute when people put coins in the slot. I used to watch them, mesmerized, until sheer panic consumed me when I didn't know where my mother had gone. She was never more than four steps away but oh, the ocean of tears that fell from my eyes until I turned in her direction and found her!

I have been an adult for a long time now and I've lost my mother, again. Some might think that was careless of me. This time, however, we are not in the grocery store. When I dial her number, a series of beeps and a recorded message remind me that it has been disconnected or is no longer in service. I mindlessly walk to the car, about to drive across town to the nursing home where I saw her last, before remembering that there's now a stranger lying in her bed.

Where has she gone?

My grown-up mind recalls her funeral and the words I spoke to honor her. Many words, all uttered on the outbreath of love.

But where is she now?

I've never been on this good earth without her.

Maybe it is I who am lost.

Or maybe she is still no farther than four steps away from me. Perhaps it is she who tucks the down comforter under my chin as I sleep. It is also she who has joined my Dad, as heavenly parking attendants, in opening the first space for me whenever I visit the mall.

Could it be that she is close behind me, arms wrapped 'round me like a warm, woolen cape? When I turn, so does she. Gone from my sight but not from my life.

I haven't lost her.

She is with me. Always and forever.

Celebration Conflagration

John Sheffield

The day after her husband walked out, Maryanne made a bonfire of his clothes and favorite possessions in her backyard. On a hot summer's evening, she stripped to her underwear, poured a large gin and tonic, and danced around the blaze, glass in hand, singing the first verse of a favorite Tony Bennett song, "I Wanna Be Around."

She couldn't remember the next few lines and took a swig of her drink. She hadn't noticed that an errant cinder had spread the fire to dry grass at the edge of the lot. The smoke stung her eyes. She didn't linger to sing the final chorus. She went indoors and refreshed her gin and tonic, which was quickly followed by a third one.

Meanwhile, the blaze spread to some bushes and from there to the edge of the driveway, where it soon set fire to the tires on her car. The exploding gas tank alerted Maryanne to the problem and she rushed to the window to see flames shooting from the car and a flaming stream of gasoline heading across the road. Panic penetrating her alcoholic haze, Maryanne grabbed her purse and rushed out a side door. She called the emergency line on her cell and was put on hold. By the time she got through and, panic stricken, told about the fire, a house across the street had caught fire along with the gas main and another car's gas tank.

The whole street was ablaze when the first fire truck arrived and firemen began to contain the inferno. The police removed everyone from the subdivision. Fortunately, no one was injured. The second fire truck arrived and set to work.

The firemen were absorbed in dealing with the subdivision's problems and didn't see that the fire had moved into the woods that bordered Maryanne's backyard and separated her house from a plastics factory. A monstrous explosion soon caught their attention and the third and fourth fire trucks were diverted to deal with the new problem.

These trucks arrived too late to assist the site's fire crew and prevent the factory's destruction. In its death throes the factory shot flaming balls of plastics across the whole area, setting fire to the neighboring town.

The police, having moved the subdivision's inhabitants to a local school, worked to find out what had happened. Their attention soon focused on Maryanne, and a detective took her to see the chief.

"What the hell happened?" he asked.

Maryanne pointed into the distance. "My husband made me do it," she replied, and sang the last verse of "I Wanna Be Around."

Fired
Terry Segal

I've just been let go from my job of twenty-five years. Boom. Like that. There may have been some warning signs that I ignored. I got a gold watch, and a Mother's Day card, but the anvil didn't drop until we drove away, leaving our youngest child at college. That's when it happened. Fired as Mommy.

Oh, I'm sure that "Mom" will be called back in for the odd job here and there, but gone is the honored position of Boo-boo Kisser, Lunch Packer, Clay Volcano Maker, Laundry Queen, and Chief Cook and Bottle Washer.

They were twenty-five years of excellent service. I planned trips to the beach and the mountains. We changed time zones. I brought hard-boiled eggs and a makeshift potty. I schlepped swimsuits and sweaters, sunscreen and scarves.

How did this sneak up on me? I told our daughter when we unpacked the car at college that once they discover that she's only eleven years old, they will send her home.

But she isn't and they won't.

I catch the eye of other pink-slip Mommies and we recognize each other's wet, blank stare. It's a combination of grief that this phase of life has passed so quickly, with the joy of a job well done. It also holds the thought that we'd better not blink again, because that's what moves the hands around the clock with such great speed.

Our daughter begins her next adventure and I begin mine, separately, for the first time. My husband and I continue our journey, still together, but alone again, different now, with the nest too empty.

It's not the same for Daddies, though. Daddies don't get fired. They're needed in much the same ways as before. But for us, Mommies? The prayed-for silence is instantly deafening. The flurry of activities comes to a screeching halt. We realize that the only pair of undies on the floor is our own, and that we were the chargers into which everyone else was plugged.

Following that fleeting moment of freedom upon being fired, is a crushing hollowness that only anotherMommy can truly understand.

OTHERWORLDLY

The Story of Changing Woman — **Terry Segal**

The Dance of the Martian Dragonflies — **John Sheffield**

Under a Bucket — **Carolyn Robbins**

Turn Off the Noise — **Terry Segal**

The Story of Changing Woman

Terry Segal

Once upon a time, just last week, Margie, a woman in her forties sat at her kitchen table, massaging her temples with her fingertips, in a circular motion.

"I'm overwhelmed," she sighed.

Her husband, Jeff, on his way into the living room to watch the football game, asked, "Why are you overwhelmed? You're off-duty. Sophie's asleep and the other two are out." He lifted his bowl of buttery popcorn and the frosty, brown bottle of beer in his hand. "Want to join me?"

Margie snorted a laugh and shook her head. "No thanks. Sophie's only four years old and taking a nap. It's not like she's in college. That doesn't exactly qualify me to be 'off duty.' And the village is raising the other two but only until lacrosse practice and hip-hop are over. Then I'm the warden again."

"I'm here," he said, pounding his chest with the beer bottle and almost spilling the popcorn all over the floor. "I'll watch everyone and the game. Why don't you go take a nap?"

"I'm not going to waste my time off sleeping. I wish I could go for a walk in the woods."

"Then why don't you?" he said.

"Because I could trip and fall or get Lyme disease and then I'd be out of commission. The warrior of the world can't take sick days."

"Oh, okay." He shrugged his shoulders. "So you're good?"

Margie nodded and dismissed him with a wave of her hand. "I'm great."

Jeff left the room and then leaned his head back in through the doorway. "Hey, Marge, what are we having for dinner?"

"I don't know. Maybe I'll forage for berries," she said.

He disappeared into the next room where his new toy, the big-screen TV, awaited.

Margie thought, *I wish screaming at sweaty men on TV relaxed me like it does him.* She raised her arms overhead and stretched back in her chair, trying to open her rib cage so she could take a deep breath. *I think the last deep breath I took was twenty years ago at my college graduation.* She drew in a short breath and audibly exhaled. *It's been a blur of activity since then.* Suddenly, a burst of energy jolted her from the seat.

"I *will* go for a walk in the woods!"

Jeff was yelling at the players so Margie decided to scrawl a note to him on her signature pink heart paper. "In search of myself. Be back soon, whether I find me or not. Love, Me…please."

She slipped out through the back door and stepped into her red gardening clogs that Sophie called her "clown shoes." She moved off the patio, past the swing set, and traversed the tree line into the magic of the woods. There was a crisp breeze that tousled her hair and made her feel free. Her shoulders dropped away from her ears. The damp air carried the musky scent of startled skunk and she experienced the perfect order of the Universe, contained in the cacophony of the surrounding creatures. Her clogs padded along the slick, brown leaves that once were painted in vibrant hues.

They remind me of me, she thought. *Vitality subdued.*

"Who are you?" a high-pitched voice shrieked, shocking her as it pierced the silence of her thoughts.

She looked up through the thinning treetops, in the direction of the voice, but there was only a hawk circling.

Hawks are messengers. She cupped her hands around her mouth and called upward. "What missive do you have for me?"

"Who are you?" She heard it again. It sounded urgent and seemed to come from behind her this time.

She spun around, into a stance like one of the defensive linemen Jeff was watching.

"Margie!" She yelled to no one. She stood straight and tall listening for a response.

There was none.

"Forget the threat of Lyme disease. I'm losing my marbles," she said under her breath.

Rays of sun split around the trunks of the trees that surrounded her and she watched dust particles float on a beam of light. "So this is where lint is born. No doubt it will follow me home to be vacuumed."

Her attention shifted to the fiery orb of sunshine that glinted off the edge of her diamond engagement ring that nestled against the solid gold wedding band. "I've worn this for eighteen years," she said as she tilted her hand from side to side to admire the dancing rays of light. "Through many changes," she continued. "Lean times when we were first married, swollen pregnancy sausage fingers…a lot of changes. There are many facets of the 'Me' diamond that I never even stop to look at anymore." She exhaled deeply and walked along the path, soft ground gently giving way beneath her clown shoes.

"Who am I?" She looked up, as if answering the question that still hung in the air. "I am Guardian-of-the-Planet Margie, Wife Margie, and Mommy Margie. There used to be more facets than there are now."

She stubbed her toe on a rock and realized that she had stumbled upon part of an abandoned Medicine Wheel. She looked at the sacred hoop, symbolic of the never-ending cycle of life. The combination of intrigue with Native American folklore and a crush on Mr. Gibson, her high school social studies teacher, had led her to study Native traditions. This wheel was sparsely outlined in rocks and pinecones. She looked in the direction of the sun to figure out which way was east. Inviting the animal spirits to offer their wisdom on her search, she walked the wheel, thinking about how far away from herself she had gotten and how alone she felt with the responsibilities of her life.

Standing in the center of the circle, she kicked off her clogs and stamped her feet in the crunchy leaves to feel more grounded. She sensed the current of the ancestors running up from Grandmother Earth through the bottoms of her feet, through her body and out at the crown of her head, toward Grandfather Sky.

Facing east, she stated, "I wish I could depend on others to help me. I do too much myself." She called upon Golden Eagle to assist with surveying the issue from way above it. The perspective showed her that she had focused so much time and energy on making a home and a life with Jeff and the kids that she forgot about herself. She recalled the things that used to thrill and fill her with passion and joy.

Wife and Mommy were only two facets of the "Me" diamond. She remembered Forgotten Child, who used to pump her legs back and forth on the swing and ascend above the horizon. She smiled at the way the wind would plaster her hair back when the swing went forward and then, when she reversed the direction, it did, too, blowing across her cheeks and eyes. Forgotten Child was also the one who painted without a plan, danced without a style, and cooked pie by arranging sleeves of crème-filled cookies on a lining of graham cracker crust.

"I love her," Margie squealed. "I miss her, too."

Moving back to the center of the circle, she thanked Golden Eagle before facing the south and the Red Coyote. "Coyote medicine is harsh," she whispered. She walked the wheel until she saw how serious she had become, how vigilant and responsible. "I've inadvertently fostered so much dependence on me that every moment is bound up in serving others." She threw her head back and howled like Red Coyote. "I hear you howling at me," she shouted into the wind. She laughed, recalling how Wiley Coyote from her childhood cartoons always did things that backfired and blew up in his face.

Margie took a few steps forward to the center of the circle, and thanked Red Coyote for showing her the balance she needed. Facing the west and the Black Bear, she observed a desire to crawl into the cave of introspection. *Maybe I'll just find a sturdy tree to befriend and rest against it for a moment,* she thought.

Eyelids heavy, she sat on the earth at the base of a tree and let her spine meld with the rough bark at its trunk. She closed her eyes, feeling as if she had not slept in decades. Tension left her body like mercury released from the confines of a thermometer that had been dropped on a tile floor.

All was silent.

Time passed until she awakened to the feeling that she was not alone.

Fully alert, with eyes wide open, Margie heard loud rustling in the brush. She saw what she thought was a coyote. "Maybe it's just a lost dog," she uttered through short breaths, trying to comfort herself. She searched her memory for what to do when encountering a coyote. *Make noise and run? Remain silent and still?* She couldn't remember. She squinted her eyes, unable to tell if it were a wild animal watching her or just her imagination running wild.

Suddenly, the creature sprinted away, deeper into the woods. Margie saw a bushy tail that transformed into the ponytail of an old woman.

"Wait!" She called to her. "Who are you?"

The old woman turned and tilted her head down. Then she appeared as a small girl wearing a wig and the mask of a crone. Head tilted up, she looked old. Head down, it seemed as if she had the twinkly eyes of a child who mocked her, like Coyote.

"Who are you?" Margie repeated.

"Now it's you who are asking," the child/woman replied. "I'm Changing Woman."

Margie stared at her, unsure if she were dreaming.

The woman continued speaking. "You are safe. I won't harm you. You see, I *am* you, and I'm me, and all women. We are one; all facets of the same beautiful diamond."

A deep sense of peace engulfed Margie.

Changing Woman smiled and unfurled her ponytail. Her hair became a drape around her body. A wind blew and she flew, right before Margie's eyes, up into the trees and then away.

Margie noticed the chill in the air and the setting sun. *I need to get home,* she thought, as she walked across the Medicine Wheel. "Oh, I didn't even face north and the White Buffalo that brings the gift of illumination." She looked up at the darkening sky. "It's okay. I've been given a gift already," she said, and moved quickly through the woods. There were no signs of Hawk, Golden Eagle, Red Coyote, the little girl or Changing Woman. Only her footprints appeared on the dirt path as she passed through the clearing toward her backyard.

Jeff was walking toward her, arms raised in victory.

"The Bills won!" he shouted. "Buffalo does it again."

Margie laughed, delighted to know that Buffalo had appeared anyway, for completion.

Jeff put his arm around her and kissed her forehead. "I was getting worried because you were gone for so long. I was afraid you had run away from home."

Margie's thoughts turned from her adventures to the chores ahead, making dinner and monitoring homework.

"Did you find yourself?" Jeff asked softly.

They had arrived at the glass sliding door on their patio. Jeff made a point to enter first, and then swept his arm up in a grand gesture toward the table, as if he were Vanna White presenting a winning vowel. He had made dinner.

"Ta-da!" he announced proudly, revealing a table set with paper plates, hotdogs, buns, beans, pickles, and Sophie in her place, smiling.

"Wow." Margie was stunned. "My childhood comfort food. Thank you, dear."

Mandy, their eldest daughter, emerged from the kitchen holding a bowl filled with salad.

"I made it." She beamed.

"That's wonderful," Margie told her. "All of it," she said to Jeff.

"Jason, close your books now. It's time for dinner," Jeff told their son.

"Mom, I just finished my report," he said grinning, holding a folder in the air. "Dad helped me."

Margie smiled as she looked down at the open book on the side of the table. Across the top of the page it read: *The Navajo Story of Changing Woman*. She felt chills on her whole body. She scanned the words. "Changing Woman came after First Man and First Woman and matured in four days. She carries the powers of rejuvenation. Her presence is symbolic of the cycle of the earth each year, renewing itself in spring and slowly dying with winter's arrival, before beginning again in a pattern of seasonal rebirth in the spring that follows."

Margie flushed with the shock of recognition that she had changed and because she had shifted and transformed, those who walk in her circle had shifted as well. She turned toward Jeff and whispered in his ear. "Thank you, dear. I did find myself, along with a beautiful, many-faceted diamond."

She took her seat at the table, acknowledging the help that she had received from all directions. Margie whispered a prayer of gratitude for the connection of her spirit to the spirit of all women. She knew deep in her heart, that she would never again feel alone in her role as a woman.

The Dance of the Martian Dragonflies
John Sheffield

The smooth red plain curves gently
Up the canyons to the distant mountains.
The night in cold stillness
Retreats and merges with their silhouettes.

The sun's heat drives down this special day
Through the tenuous atmosphere,
And cuts into the frozen surface, biting deep.
This is the millennium.

The rays release trapped vapors.
In turn, they trap the heat.
Exploding out of the ground, the pressure fronts
Howl down the rilles, valleys and ravines.

The winds scour the dust from forgotten river beds.
The surface of the planet struggles.
The tearing clouds spread out across the surface.
Winds collapse. Gentle clouds envelop the mountains.

In the still atmosphere, the glistening chrysalides
Lie warming on the red earth.
Warm hours pass and the chrysalides unfold.
A gentle murmur wafts over the plains.

The Martian dragonflies rise slowly,
Spreading fragile, translucent wings to dry.
Softly they beat upward into the sky.
A cloud of movement the warm day through.

In long remembered choreography they dance,
Pairing off before curling to the ground.
On the warm earth in the setting sun
They mate and die.

The cold darkness of space settles onto Mars,
Pulling back the vapor like a cloak.
Shielding the nascent dragonflies in a blanket of ice.
Frozen, life suspended for another thousand years.

Under a Bucket

Carolyn Robbins

"According to the computer there are five of us signed up for this *Historical engineering of ancient machines* Class. I'm Martin Jenkins, who's Alan Wolcott?" He scanned the cavernous room.

A voice echoed out from behind a series of metal shelves. A short, tubby, twentyish-man made his way out of the shadows carrying a boxed circular saw, which he waved in the air. "That's me. Look what I found. This could come in handy."

A deep booming voice from near the door asked, "Professor, you got a Josh Nelson on your list?"

"Yes, but you misunderstood this gray hair. I'm not a professor or the advisor, just one of the students."

A surprised look appeared on Nelson's face. "Sorry, who are the other two?"

"I'm Sammy Chu," said the scrawny guy in a white lab coat, sitting cross-legged on the floor with his i-Pad glowing on his lap. "And the missing one is Cal Black. He is now ten minutes and twenty-five seconds late.

Light flooded in from above and a thunderous bang of a metal door hitting another piece of metal stopped their conversation. Everyone squinted up into the light. A figure was silhouetted in the open doorway at what would have been the second floor above a span of steel support girders.

"You Cal Black?" Josh asked.

Sammy said, "Whoever you are, I wouldn't take a step, 'cause there's no floor up there and it's a long first step down."

"Thanks. Yeah, I'm Cal."

Alan's voice squeaked, "Cal's a girl."

"No kidding slick." Josh shook his head at Alan, and waved at the door behind him. "Cal, come in this door down here."

"Okay. By the way, Cal's short for Calista." She leaned forward into the gloom of the basement shop. The large shop lights above her head back-lit her jet black hair with highlights. "Guys, how do I get down there?"

The loose jeans and oversized T-shirt she wore did little to hide her form. In fact, the T shirt became almost transparent under the harsh backlighting.

Martin cleared his throat, "Ah, go back to the front and take the first door to the left."

She disappeared and a moment later they heard the door click shut.

A wolf whistle came from the floor. "She's so stacked," Sammy whispered in awe. "I'd love to run my hands over…."

"Sammy, forget it. You wouldn't know what to do if she offered it," said Alan.

"After that brilliant comment of, 'Cal's a girl' you think you have a chance?" Sammy hooted.

Before Alan could come back with a smart reply a deep booming laugh came from Josh, "Guys, you're nuts if any of you think we could get so much as a smile from her. If she does smile, it won't be because she impressed, it'll be because she laughing at us. Face it, we're nerds."

"Geez, how do you think she managed to get into this class?" Alan asked. He stared at all of his fellow classmates. "Those prerequisites, I barely had enough to get into this class. How could a *girl* do it?"

"Good point, but how the hell did you get past the eight hours of PE requirement?" Josh asked staring at Alan's obvious girth. Ignoring his own question, he added reverently. "On the other hand, she looked in great shape."

"I suppose you had an easy time with being fluent in one of the ancient language choices?" Alan asked as he shoved his black-rimmed glasses up on his head.

"Gentlemen, we can argue all day about each of our capabilities, but it won't accomplish much," Martin said. "Let's wait for Cal and we can exchange our pedigrees then."

Josh Nelson leaned against a drill press. "Works for me. To pass the time, anyone want to bet on how long it will take for her to find us?"

Sammy Chu barely looked up from the glowing screen in his lap. "I'll put up ten on an hour." He yanked out a ten-dollar bill and waved it in the air.

"How 'bout odds on how long it will take one of us to get her out of those jeans?" Alan asked.

"That's what I call optimism." Martin raised an eyebrow.

"I never give up."

The door behind them clicked.

Josh hooted, "Easy money, I got it, sucker." He grabbed the ten out Sammy's hand and stuffed it in his pocket just as the door swung open.

Cal rushed into the room heading toward Martin, dust motes swirling behind her. "Okay, I'm here. Sorry about that professor, I couldn't find this place. What have I missed?"

Martin smiled, and thought she was adorable. "Actually, nothing. According to this computer the whole class has arrived, and it has instructions for all five of us." He waved his hand to include all of them.

"You're not our advisor?"

"He's a student, Cal," Sammy said from his spot on the floor. "It seems the computer is our advisor. What we have to do is on *it*."

Cal, Josh, and Alan leaned over the computer on the table and scanned the listed instructions. Sammy remained seated cross-legged on the cement floor, staring at his tablet.

Having read the instructions, Martin walked over to Sammy. "You've already managed to access that info?" He asked staring over his shoulder at his glowing tablet screen.

"Yeah." He glanced up at Martin staring at him. "Get used to it, I like sitting on the floor. I think better down here."

"Whatever works." Martin said.

Sammy shrugged. "According to this, we've got some serious talent in the room. Three of us hold multiple degrees." He gestured to the screen where he'd highlighted each of their names. Next to every name was a list of all the completed prerequisite requirements. "Of course, you've got us all at a disadvantage, besides a degree in history, you're a medical doctor. On the up side, if any of us gets hurt, we know who to find."

Martin glanced at everyone then back to the screen. "Right, and I know that you're the man if we need a computer geek or expert advice on Asian artifacts." He smiled. "I don't know if you've read those instructions to the end, but by the time we get to the second segment of this class we're going to have to work together."

Alan spoke up from his tablet. "I hate working with people. They always screw up. I refuse to fail because of idiots…even doctors."

Josh slapped Alan's huge back. "Cheer up. The first six weeks, we're required to work on individual projects. Each of us have to construct a device. At the beginning of the second session we are to demonstrate our machine."

"The weird thing is we're not allowed to test them until that day," Sammy added.

"I think that's so we'll have an intact machine on finals day," Martin said, rubbing his own shoulder.

Josh added, "Also, we can't take any of our machines from this room. Apparently our computer leader wants original work with no input from outside experts."

Martin said, "Okay. Continuing, they'll be judged that day and the one with the most promise will be refined by all of us. See Alan, you have time to be brilliant all by yourself."

"I'm fine with the first six weeks. Then we'll see who survives." Alan said.

Martin looked around at everyone. "I'd originally suggested we verbally give introductions to the others before we got started on our projects. However, it seems Sammy has us all listed with our credentials in his computer. Sammy, send us an email copy of your list."

In seconds the list appeared on everyone's computer screen.

Calista –Cal, Black   Degrees in Botany and Archeology- fluent in Cherokee, Egyptian hieroglyphics and a working knowledge of ancient Akkadian, and worked digs for two seasons in Turkey and Egypt.

Sammy Chu   Degrees in architecture, computer science, and Asian history. Black belt judo expert. Fluent in several ancient Japanese dialects.

Martin Jenkins, M.D., also a doctorate in History, fluent in Latin and ancient Greek.

Josh Nelson- degree in Mechanical Engineering. Fluent in the Icelandic languages; Danish, Swedish, and Norwegian.

Alan Wolcott- degrees in music and Archeology. Fluent in Welsh and Gaelic.

Martin stood. "I think we should either start studying all those blueprints and drawings on the computer or delve into that intriguing collection of manuscripts on that corner shelf. Six weeks isn't much time to get working prototypes of anything, much less a copy of an ancient machine that no one even knows will work."

Cal stared at the area that surrounded her. "At least that explains why we're in this room. From what I can see we have a machine shop, a wood working shop, I think that's chem lab equipment over there, and I can't begin to guess what's beyond that. She grinned. We have many toys to play with and I can't wait to get started." She dusted off her jeans from where she had leaned against a bench and headed over to the pile of manuscripts.

From beyond the chem lab equipment Josh spoke up. "I'd like to mention that besides some wood, metal and those chemicals, most of this stuff looks like antique discards. We've been stuck with all of the university's cast-offs."

"Damn, this class is never going to work," Alan whined.

"Could it be we have this stuff because we're supposed to be building ancient devices?" Martin asked.

"What! Just because the device is old, we have to use antique tools?" Alan said. "I won't."

Sammy smiled. "That's a good way to get out of this class. You going to drop out now that things aren't going your way?"

"Quit? Hell, no." Alan spat back at Sammy. "Wouldn't give the 'boy genius' that kind of satisfaction. I'm in for the whole class. You guys haven't got a chance."

###

Four hours later Cal left the basement carrying only her phone. Smiling to herself, she knew she'd found her project and all the records she needed were securely scanned onto it. The others had still been digging through the material when she left. What dumb luck, the first manuscript she'd picked up had notations in cuneiform. From the dig she'd worked on last summer she'd been able to read enough of what was written next to the drawings to convince herself she'd be able to build it. According to a small post-it on the corner, the manuscript had been found inside an amphora at the bottom of the sea off the coast of Alexandria. *If* she'd translated it correctly, she was going to build a Phoenician clock.

Six weeks later

The five met back in the basement for the presentation of their projects. Still no sign of a human advisor waited for them in their workroom. Only the ever-present computer screen waited with new instructions.

You will present your projects to the class in alphabetical order.

Alan grinned. "This is going to be good."

Cal grinned back, because with her name starting with a B she'd be first. She glanced at Alan's smug face suspecting he thought his place as last in line was a perfect position. Over the six weeks Alan's ego had become an irritant for everyone. But for some reason, he disliked her presence more than anyone. She could sense that he was anticipating that moment when she would crash and be kicked from the final project. Cal smiled because she believed her clock would work. More than anything she wanted to prove Alan wrong.

Cal positioned herself in front of the group. "As you know I've been working on a plan for an ancient timepiece. I finished it last night. A moment ago I wound the spring and now I'm going to engage this ruby pin." She waved a small tapered ruby at them.

Holding the time piece in front of her, she first inserted and then pushed on the small red jewel. A whirring sound filled the room, she felt as if she were being spun around, and around with the old shop lights swirling past her blurring everything. Next a dark cloud enveloped her. It was scary. She stifled a scream determined to remain calm in front of the guys.

Dizzy, she closed her eyes. Her stomach lurched. Abruptly, the spinning stopped. She tried to regain her balance and calm her stomach. Through her mild nausea Cal heard two women screaming. *What's going on? I'm the only woman in the room.*

Prying open her eyes she discovered she was no longer in the university basement. She stood in a rustic barnyard complete with chickens pecking at her bare feet. *Bare feet? She glanced down. Where'd her shoes go? Oh, my God, I'm stark naked. What have I gotten myself into?*

Cal looked up. Eight feet away stood two terrified women. They were dressed in perfect replicas of seventeenth century dresses, one blue and the other dove gray. The one in gray held a dripping wooden water bucket with a bouquet of wildflowers in it.

The other woman held her arms crossed in front of her body. "Be gone you unclean, evil witch. Be gone."

As she stared at the one in pale blue it dawned on her that perhaps the dresses weren't replicas. She considered a new premise. Could she have traveled in time? Cal looked back down. While her feet were pretty muddy, the rest of her was clean looking, so she didn't deserve the tag of unclean. Her error was she lacked a single stitch of clothing. Embarrassed, she tried to cover herself. It was only then that what the women screamed at her sunk in. She had a bigger problem than indecency. They thought she was a witch. If she'd time traveled and this was still New England, she'd be burned at the stake by sunset. Yes, she had a huge problem.

"Oh, damn." Cal said. *Oh, no, I shouldn't have said damn.*

As if to confirm her thoughts the woman in the blue dress shouted, "Hester, cover her head with your bucket. We can't allow her devil eyes to gaze on us. She could bewitch us."

"Ah, I've got to leave," Cal said. She looked down and her hands fumbled with her time machine. When she glanced back up it was just in time to see the woman swing her bucket up. Cal desperately pushed and pulled on the ruby pin.

With a thunk, the bucket landed on her head just as she felt her body begin to spin. Again darkness surrounded her. This time she was delighted to be in the dark.

She stopped spinning.

Dizzy, Cal drew a deep breath to steady herself. She wondered if she was okay and did a quick physical inventory to answer that question. Holding onto the bucket on her head, she felt cold, otherwise she seemed to be okay. The big question was *where was she?*

"Damn Cal, that's one hell of an entrance." Josh said. "Where have you been?"

From on the floor Sammy said, "Alan, you were right that first day of class. Cal is very definitely a girl. The view from down here is awesome."

She was back.

"I've got a better question. Why are you naked with a bucket on your head?" Alan asked.

Pulling the bucket off her head with one hand while staring in amazement at her timepiece, she said, "Shit, I didn't build a clock."

Sitting at her feet, Sammy murmured, "Your flowers look great."

She shivered. "Sammy, would you lend me your lab coat? And stop staring as if you'd never seen a woman."

Her reprimand didn't change his rapt expression, but he did manage to stand and hand her his coat.

Alan chortled, "I knew you'd screw up. What's with the flowers in your hair?"

"Thanks." She said to Sammy. As she yanked the coat on, she added. "Alan, It worked. I just didn't know *what* I was building. I built a time machine."

Clutching the coat around her, she glanced at her classmates. "Guys, I learned something important, when you travel through time it's dangerous. Your modern clothes don't go with you and people tend to think you're a witch."

Turn Off the Noise

Terry Segal

Turn off the noise.

Listen for the whispering of angels.

They call to you over the din of technology, the television that plays to no one,
under the guise of company, and the radio, with its hypnotic repetition.

Quiet your cell phone. De-program yourself from high alert each time a friend shares a thought.

Be unafraid of silence.

Step away from your computer. Its screen saver signals when the device is at rest.

Do you rest?

Let an angelic image serve as your soul saver, lest you forget to unplug from the chaos of each day.

Disentangle from the web of the world and let the wind carry you outside.

Run, before it's too late.

Breathe.

And listen…

Stand beneath the canopy of stars in the ink jet sky.

Feel the mist on your face like the earth's thirsty flowers.

Plant your feet firmly in the garden and stretch yourself toward the heavens.

Hear the ancient drumming of rain upon sacred land.

Discern the sound of the winged ones, whether bird, butterfly, fairy or angel.

Drop tense shoulders that plug your ears.

Listen for rustling wings through the chambers of your heart.

Angels are close by and here to help.

Some guard, some heal, some protect and all serve.

Ask for guidance. Then listen for their reply.

Humor-2

Ulysses Returned	**John Sheffield**
Corporal Punishment – A Lament	**Tom Leidy**
Dirty Dudley's	**John Sheffield**
The Gorilla	**John Sheffield**

Ulysses Returned

John Sheffield

James Joyce's novel Ulysses *is not an easy read. The author engages in literary stunts, seemingly because he feels he can get away with them, for example, a half page of adjectives describing a man, ultra-long sentences, and many languages. Nevertheless, I enjoyed his showing off his literary skills. This parody is my homage to his genius.*

Grasping the copy of James Joyce's *Ulysses* and his best cane with the silver ferrule and horn handle, he headed out the door of the retirement home bent on reaching the library safely. He ignored the cooing sounds of the blue-haired harpy, who waited Circe-like in her seat by the front door, hoping to trap an unsuspecting male. Typical of the women here, she undoubtedly had her butt secured by elasticated bonds—enough of the material in the retirement home to cover the Hindenburg, he suspected. If only it would suffer the fate of that airship…*illegitimi carborundum* or something similar in pig-Latin. A passing memory of his long-departed wife brought tears to his eyes. She had never worn a bum-crusher—her words. None of the women here could compensate for her absence—the lack of companionship, cuddling, no elastic holding the body together. Nothing to do with sex. He would press on regardless; *omnia vincit perseverando* was his old school's motto.

    Outside, he made his way tip-tapping along the sidewalk. He turned left at the southern end of a street with a row of dining establishments and shops. Little boxes all done up in…. He couldn't remember the words to the song and contented himself with humming a bit of the tune.

A drink would be nice, but it was lunchtime and every restaurant was packed. Not going to get suffocated in a crowded bar. *Overpopulated.* The Chinese came to mind.

Bar, no the mandarin Chinese *bā*, flat tone means eight, *bà* with a down tone is father, *bǎ* down and then up is handle, *bá* up-tone means to pull out. No wonder the Chinese had so many people. Just imagine if a woman got the tones wrong, "No honey, I've got a headache" might sound like, "The time is right." God help the Cantonese with their sixteen tones.

He looked both ways and crossed the street. A careless car screeched to a stop. He waved his cane at the young woman driver. *May she broaden out to need a bum-crusher.* He made a short hop onto the safety of the sidewalk to indicate his relief at escaping death, only to feel something brush past him. The guilty party, a cyclist, tilted and fell sideways onto a low wall.

The middle-aged cyclist staggered to his feet. He wore a brown shirt flapping outside stained corduroy trousers with bicycle clips at the ankles and dirty sneakers. With one hand holding his side, he raised the other and made a fist. "You should watch where you're going, you stupid old man."

Cane raised in defense, he replied. "You shouldn't be on the sidewalk, and learn some manners."

The cyclist snorted, remounted, and sped off, turning right at the lights on the road that led down to a bridge over the river. Not the Styx with Charon to let him cross in a boat. *God, may he fall in.* Let it be the gray, green, greasy, limpid Limpopo with its gray, green crocodiles. *Chomp, chomp.* Bicycle and dirty clothes all gone in an instant.

He crossed the road when the lights changed and tapped his way around the outskirts of what had once been the gardens of a stately home. Reaching the library, he mounted the steps and, ready to face the harpies, came upon the automatic doors. They opened, a Scylla and

Charybdis waiting to trap the unwary traveler. He raised his cane to ward off the evil beings and advanced, ferrule thrust forward, into the vestibule. Turning right he arrived at the counter.

A young women came up, and said, "Can I help you?" Her name, he noticed, was Penelope.

He proffered the book and his library card. "Ulysses is late…again," he replied, having a passing concern that Ulysses being two weeks overdue might lead to weeping and wailing on her part.

Penelope showed no sign that she understood the literary allusion and scanned his card. "That will be one dollar and seventy cents," she said without a smile.

He handed over the money, momentarily unhappy she hadn't berated him for failing to pick up the bread and milk that the real Penelope might have sent him out to get.

Penelope walked away to deal with another customer. Nice butt, he thought. No elastic there. *Quelles miches* as the French would say, a reference to the curves of a farmhouse loaf.

With *Ulysses* returned and encouraged that not all women had gone to the dogs, he braved the doors without using his cane and headed home, ready to face the harpies.

Corporal Punishment – A Lament

Tom Leidy

My grandfather on my mother's side was a Freemason, and a member of the Improved Order of Redmen (IORM), the Knights of Pythias (K of P), The Independent Order of Odd Fellows (IOOF), and probably a few other lodges or tribes or counsels I don't remember or never knew about.

My grandmother and their spinster daughter (my aunt Essie) also were members of related women's auxiliaries: The Order of the Eastern Star (OES), The Degree of Pocahontas, (D of P), the White Shrine, Rebekah, etc.

Maybe, oldest and for a long time the only grandchild, before formal events I was often recruited to help set up folding chairs in the lodge hall, then put them away afterward. In between I had to watch middle-aged men wearing black suits and small aprons or middle-aged women in white floor-length gowns and tiaras march solemnly through their "stations" and recite complicated, though vaguely familiar, oaths and promises, like caring for the sick and elderly or honoring the flag. To an eight-year-old boy, the affairs were colossal bores.

The only compensation I ever enjoyed from these efforts were after-ceremony sodas or milkshakes in one or another local confectionary: Kuster's, the 400 Shoppe, or the Busy Bee. And once I was given some no-longer-required ritual pieces from Pocahontas ceremonies: a bow (no arrows) and a baseball bat too small for regulation games but ideal for a street game we called "Move-Up." The only equipment required to play Move-Up was a bat and a tennis ball.

In the 1940's our neighborhood lay on the far northwest side of town. A small patch of woods curled behind Beaky Jackson's house. Immediately west of our brick-paved streets, across a wooden bridge, past a dilapidated horse barn, a dirt road trailed a few hundred yards into open country, then faded away. Cut through by Log Pond Run flowing south and east, empty acreage stretched north and west far into the Welsh Hills and the TB sanitarium. Kids in our neighborhood feared the foamy effluent collecting around eddies in the creek was sputum from TB patients and would be instantly fatal if touched.

Our comparatively isolated location, that many mothers were working and some fathers were far away, that gasoline was rationed and precious, all left us kids pretty much to our own devices afternoons and evenings after school and weekends. Move-Up was one such device.

The game was best played on a tree-lined residential street with sidewalks and curbs on each side. At least four players were required: batter, catcher, pitcher, and as many fielders as the street could hold. The batter's objective was simply to stay at the bat. The objective for all other players was to move the batter "out" by catching a hit ball on the fly or first bounce, thus moving the batter into the field and all other players "up" a step closer to the bat.

A skilled player could hold his position by caroming the ball off a nearby tree, ricocheting it off a curb, laying down a swinging bunt, or hitting the ball really hard toward the weakest, closest fielder.

Donnie Raye lived across the street from my house with his mother. He was a sweet little boy, too young for Move-Up and prone to get into trouble, often in public view. Donnie's finest moment was the day the Raye's toilet had to be replaced. While a new unit was installed, the broken one stood in front of the house. That afternoon everyone saw Donnie sitting on the broken unit, relieving himself.

One summer evening, too dark for Move-Up and too early for older kids to come out to play Ring-Up or Kick the Can or whatever more intimate games they could think of, five of us were sitting on my front porch steps drinking not-quite-cool enough Kool Aid and talking of the events of the day when we heard scuffling in the alley and occasional cries and wails.

A moment later we saw Mrs. Raye walking out of the alley under the streetlight. She was holding Donnie by his shoulder with one hand and every two or three steps swatting him with the other hand in the general area of his behind.

"I told you, Donnie, never to pick up dead things!" (Swat! Swat!)

"I didn't know it was dead, Mommie! I didn't know!" ("Wah! Wah!")

They crossed the street, disappeared into their house, and for a moment my front porch was quiet. Then Beaky Jackson spoke. His voice was soft, his words hesitant, as if he was reluctant to say anything.

Beaky had moved to our neighborhood a few weeks earlier from West Virginia and had quickly become the leader of our little coterie. His father, Gudgel, a brakeman on the B&O railroad, often was away from home. "When I need a whuppin,'" Beaky mused, "Maw sends me out to the woods to cut a switch and uses it on me when I come back."

Don Betz's mother was a widow. He said he never got spanked; that his mother made him stay in his room till she told him he could come out. Their dad did all the Mann brothers' spanking. I said I got spanked more often by my mom, but my dad hit a lot harder. Besides Don Betz, whom we didn't quite believe, we all agreed, one way or another, we got spanked about once a week.

My dad was a big, strong, talented, intense man. I was none of these. We had little in common. At dinner he often regaled me, my mom, and my brother with the events of his day at work—venting his spleen on all the dipshits and nincompoops making his life there miserable.

Sunday afternoons (some sort of self-therapy, I suppose) he worked on various projects in his shop in the basement, but his tools—brushes, rulers, hammers, etc.—were always scattered through the house. About the only times Dad and I spent together were those Sunday afternoons. While he worked I sat on the basement stairs and we listened to mystery and thriller programs on his little radio: *The Mysterious Stranger*, *The Hermit's Cave*, *Suspense*, *Inner Sanctum*, and *Quiet Please*.

The one moment of real father-son interaction I remember clearly was the day he told me it'd be okay to pee in the coal bin. And then we did it together. "Never tell your mom," he said. I didn't, and often after, knowing it probably was a spankable offense, went out of my way to pee in the coal bin.

My cousin, Martin, and I often went to midnight movies downtown. (We called them "spook shows.") Our theaters were The Arcade and The Grand. Mart's older brother, Bob, usually drove us to the shows in his Model A sedan, but we had to get home on our own.

The movie that most affected me was *Dracula*—particularly the scene in which the count invites Renfield up the broad marble stairs to dinner in his chambers. Dracula glides mysteriously through heavy spider webs hanging low over the stairs, but Renfield gets tangled in them and must cut his way through with his umbrella.

Martin lived on Mount Vernon Road where it intersected my street. Walking home from a spook show wasn't too bad when we were together. But after Mart went inside I was on my own, two blocks away from my house down a scary, dark, tree-lined street and every night sound, every dog bark or bird rustle, signaled my certain doom. Sure one or another of the monsters and fiends we'd been watching was just behind, I'd run from one large maple tree to the next and scrunch my back tight against it. Thus protected, I'd catch my breath, build my courage, scan for monsters, then run again to the next tree, then the next and the next till I was home . . . finally safe.

Like most houses then, ours was heated with coal. Though easily available and inexpensive, it had some drawbacks. Heated air rising through the ducts carried with it into living areas microscopic ash that would cling to and discolor walls and ceilings and collect as black cobwebs festooned high in the corners of rooms, hallways, and stairwells.

Even though it was well lit and my parents were just below, ominous, black webs draped from the ceiling in the stairwell up to my bedroom terrified me. (The bathroom was upstairs, too. It was lucky I could pee in the coalbin.) And one evening I just couldn't handle it.

"Go to bed, Son!" (Angry)

"I don't want to." (Crying)

"Dammit, boy! Get up to bed! Tomorrow's a school day! Move! (Really angry!)

"No! No!" (Really crying!)

I didn't see Dad hurry into the dining room where he'd been hanging pictures and grab his yardstick. But suddenly there he was and he whacked me hard with it all the way up the stairs into my room. Not one of those bendable things sold out of bins today in warehouse stores, Dad's yardstick was heavy, inflexible.(He always used the best quality tools.) It hurt like hell . . . and it cured me of the apparent symptoms of my stairwell phobia. And, as with the trees in the night, I learned to slither upstairs, my back pressed securely against the wall.

When I was about ten I spent a lot of time building flying model airplanes. Long hours spent in my closed bedroom with balsa wood, tissue, glue and airplane "dope" often left me a little woozy.

Finished, flying models always looked good (except for their too-large propellers) standing on the dresser or hanging from the ceiling, but were disappointing otherwise. Either they didn't fly well, turned over and spiraled straight to the ground; or they flew too well, into a tree or onto the roof of the garage. Eventually, I found a solution to the problem. I'd squirt airplane glue on a finished model, light it up, and fly it burning out the window of my parents' bedroom to the backyard two stories below.

One afternoon, after arranging the satisfactory immolation of a German Focke-Wulf 190, as I was leaving the bedroom I saw my mother's hand mirror on her dressing table. She had used it on me many times, but I was surprised then to realize I hadn't been spanked in maybe a month or more, and thought I might be beginning to grow up and wouldn't be spanked again . . . an enlightened, exhilarating feeling. And mostly, I wasn't.

All this happened a long time ago. My old neighborhood no longer lies on the edge of town. The broad fields and pastures west have been replaced by new developments, shopping plazas, and crowded four-lane traffic. Aunt Essie, Grandma and Granddad, Mom and Dad, Beaky, the Mann brothers, Don Betz, my cousins, and my brother . . . all are gone. The Move-Up bat disappeared somehow, somewhere along the way. The spook show theaters have been demolished. None of the confectionaries remains. Our house is there still, but the brick pavement on the street has buckled and is no longer good for games.

But, just in case, I still have Dad's yardstick.

Dirty Dudley's

John Sheffield

One of the joys of living near Oxford in the early 60s was eating at the Lamb and Flag, some ten miles southwest of the city in Longworth—a pub generally known as Dirty Dudley's. Why that epithet? Answer: Because it was dirty. From the outside, the old Cotswold stone building looked respectable. But inside, the floors looked as if they hadn't been cleaned since the eighteenth century; knowledgeable patrons always checked their plates for cracks and their cutlery for traces of ancient food. Dudley and his Amazonian wife, or possibly mistress, presided over the bar, each wearing a food- and drink-stained apron covering nearly spherical abdomens—a male and female Tweedledee and Tweedledum. The assemblies were held together by matched four-inch-wide leather belts. Dudley was a gourmand. It was said that every week he would travel to the markets in London to obtain the very best fresh produce. As evidenced by his girth, he ate a lot of his purchases.

The most remarkable feature of his pub was that you wrote your own bill. Following aperitifs, dinner, and after dinner drinks, you went to the bar and offered to pay. Dudley or his mistress would hand you a scruffy piece of paper and a pencil, and you would write down what it was you thought you might have had. The meal was relatively easy to remember: three soups, one paté, two smoked salmon, four pheasant, one lamb chops, one trout almandine, a large bowl of mixed salad, four English trifles, and two crème brulées. It was with the drinks that the memory played tricks.

"Ethel, did you have one or two medium sherries?"

"Oh *gawd*, I don't know. Better put two."

"How many bottles of burgundy did we have?"

"Definitely two."

"Got to be three. George drank one on his own. Then there was at least one bottle of Chablis."

So, while it was said that some students from the university conned the system, I am sure that most people overpaid, and Dudley never, never, never questioned their estimates of consumption. A great place to eat out for those with a strong constitution--sadly, long gone.

The Gorilla
John Sheffield

Guy, the silverback sat on the floor of his cage.

Mandarin-like, he surveyed his audience.

Staring, eyes dark and unrevealing, he held out his left hand.

Palm flat, Guy displayed a single, large orange.

Raising the orange to his mouth, he incised its pole.

His right index finger extended towards us.

With precision, the nail delicately peeled back a leaf of the peel.

From Guy, a slowly scanned glance as if to say, "Look how skillful I am."

Leaf by leaf curled down until the naked orange core lay exposed in his palm.

We watched, in awe, waiting for the surgical removal of each delicious segment.

In one instant, his mouth was agape, canines exposed. The orange inhaled.

Three chomps and all gone. The peel discarded.

Did the corner of Guy's mouth twitch? An eyebrow raise? If so, imperceptibly.

He turned and, protecting those surgeon's fingers, knuckle-sashayed into his lair.

The flower-like peel the only evidence of his practical joke.

ODDS AND ENDS

Inspirations:	Jeremy Logan
An Essay on Writing Creatively	
The Spore Family	John Sheffield
Damn Marching Bands	John Sheffield
I Believe in Failure	Megan Benoit Ratcliff
Maybe It's About the Story	Megan Benoit Ratcliff

Inspirations
An Essay on Writing Creatively
Jeremy Logan

Writing my latest novel stirred up emotion I haven't felt in decades, discovering inspiration from hidden places in my psyche that bled onto the pages. Since it was partly a "coming of age" story, I was transported to my teenage years, which reminded me of my first infatuations, early sexual fantasies, and rivalries.

One thing I had forgotten over the years is that a little sexual tension in the day can change an ordinary mood into one of optimism and inspiration. I'm not talking about the manifestation of desires, it's all about harmless flirting and thinking someone is flirting back. This is our imagination at work, transforming an innocent exchange into an inspiration of adventure that wouldn't have been there if we hadn't given into the flirtation.

I'm a guy, I act like one, oblivious and thick-skinned – but under the surface I'm a romantic. I often hide it because, quite frankly, I'm more accustomed to being around other guys, and romantic doesn't play well in that scenario. That means I have to make an effort to break the seal on the romantic in me every now and then and let it breathe. Romantic memories, imaginary or real, are one source of inspiration that have always been available to me, ready to glorify living in the moment.

Lately I've been exploring and experimenting with an hypothesis. Can a little harmless flirting be inspirational? Last month on a Saturday, my wife's day was filled with appointments and lunch with friends. I was on my own and ready to test the hypothesis. My first unsuspecting target was the lady at the dry cleaner. I've patronized the place for years and we were on a first name basis. She's an extrovert, so I knew this first attempt was going to be without stress. I walked in and she smiled at me.

"Hello Mr. Jeremy," she said as she turned from behind the counter to search for my clothes hanging from the wires in the sky. "Hi, Vivi," I responded.

I eyed her from head to toe, searching for something that might be new about her that day. I was aiming for a compliment I could give her that would be something she wouldn't expect from me. Finding nothing different, I said, "You seem mighty cheerful today," knowing perfectly well that she acted no different that day than on all of the other previous days. To my surprise, she said grinning brightly, "I do feel good today. Thanks for noticing."

Bingo! And we started flirting. About halfway into our conversation, she reached out her hand, placing it under my hand, which was resting on the counter. "I've never noticed your ruby ring before," she said. "Does it have special sentiment for you?"

She might have been trying to get a better look at it, but her touch surprised me. I was thinking she had also played this game before, knowing it would affect me, and wanting to see how I would react. We chatted for a few minutes, breaking it off when another customer walked in.

"Bye, Vivi. See you next time," I said as I picked up my clothes from the hanger rod.

"Bye-bye, Mr. Jeremy," she replied with a smile and a twinkle in her eye.

I could have stopped right there and the experiment would have been a huge success. I felt energized and emboldened to try it again. An hour later, I was sitting in my usual seat at the Atlanta Writer's Club. The president, asked the assembled, "Raise your hand if this is your first meeting." A middle-aged attractive lady sitting in front of me raised her hand. I thought to myself, *Aha, my next target.*

At the break, I stood up and paused. She did the same and looked toward the back of the room, which was right at me. I said, "I noticed you raised your hand as a new member. If you don't mind my asking, what inspired you to join?"

She smiled and said, "I've been thinking about it for long time. Are you a new member?"

And we were off. I smiled and we walked together up the aisle. She spoke with a slight accent that I believed was Portuguese, probably from Brazil. Outside in the hall we exchanged names and chatted a few minutes until some fellow author friends stopped to say hello. I introduced my new friend, Anna, to them. She seem pleased to make the acquaintance of the several authors that gathered around. One of the women authors broke away, saying she was headed for the restroom and Anna followed.

I was still standing in the same place, talking to a different author that had stepped away just as Anna approached. "Jeremy," she said. "I want to thank you for introducing me to your friends and colleagues. I never imagined it was going to be this easy to feel at home. I'm pretty shy – trying to write a little. I needed this to work out." We talked awhile and returned to our seats.

This is so easy, I thought to myself. All it took was the initiative to be friendly and outgoing. The rest of the day I had a smile inside me, ready to bloom at the slightest provocation. I couldn't help but wonder if there was a link between flirting and a cheerful disposition. That thought was followed by an epiphany. Imagination might be the difference to one's happiness. Using my own experience as my guide, I know that when my imagination is restricted or limited to fearful things, the result is a negative or protective mood. Opening my mind to imagine myself in enjoyable circumstances transforms my mood to engaging and playful prospects. How one gets to this position is the issue. If it's not your natural personality, can it be conjured up? I believe it can, but it takes initiative.

The first step is to remember to try it. The second step involves thinking of things you wish you could be doing that are enjoyable to you. The third, and last, step is to imagine how you would appear if you were engaged in the enjoyable activity. Just getting to the last step is all it takes. I'm no medical person or psychiatrist, but I imagine that endorphins are activated and released into your bloodstream that create the illusion of pleasure. Before you know it, you're hunting for real or more imagined encounters that perpetuate the feeling of exuberance.

This is the point that you, the reader, asks, "Why do you think you know this works?" I answer, "I'm in the imagination business. That's what authors do. We're constantly looking for inspiration. We need it to fuel our efforts."

For me, in order to transform an inspiration into a novel, it has to be huge and special. It has to be so big that it sustains me for an entire year. That's about how long it takes me to finish a novel. Not all my days are inspirational, but I've learned that if I keep my mind open, hunting and adventurous, I'll find it."

I've learned another beautiful thing about this process. When I've been inspired sufficiently to fuel a novel, I'm in a state of perpetual bliss. I can't wait to find time to write, and in between the times I'm writing, without knowing it, I'm opening up my mind to explore more and more possibilities.

Here's where I make apologies to my family, friends and acquaintances. I might be sitting next to you imagining. Conjuring up all sorts of things. You might be inspiring me without knowing it. If you knew what I was thinking, I hope you would approve. But in reality it's not necessary. The good part for me is that it improves my mood, my attitude and my writing. Is that selfish? It might be, so I apologize.

There is still an unanswered question – how does an inspiration turn into a literary work? On my website blog I've written about this process. For me, I go into my childhood daydream mode. One minute I'm observing something or experiencing an event – the next minute I'm imagining an alternative reality.

Here's an example: I'm sitting in a restaurant with friends when I notice a couple having an active discussion at the table beside us. I can't hear a word they're saying, and I don't read lips, so I start imagining what it's all about. I pretend the woman looks familiar. Perhaps she was an old flame twenty years ago. From there I can proceed in several directions. Let's say I invent that she left me, the dreamer, for a more practical partner. Next, I sprinkle in the ingredients needed for all entertaining stories: romance, competition, dire consequences, and the invention of characters that will captivate the reader. And if I'm writing the story, it has to have a plot filled with mystery, secrets, suspense and an unexpected conclusion.

She says to her date, "You're a lot like my first love, Jeremy. You spend more time on impractical matters and not enough time on me."

He replies, "Margaret, have you ever considered that you're only concerned about how I can please you? You're a Narcissist, no longer worthy of my love." He throws down his napkin on the table and stands up. "I'm leaving you. Have a wonderful life with yourself," he says just before he walks out of the restaurant.

To my shock, Margaret turns and looks at me. "Jeremy," she says, "I knew he wasn't right for me. I had to end it. And when I saw you sitting there I couldn't help but use the same excuse that worked on you. Thanks for inspiring me."

How about that for irony? There I was using a using my imagination to invent an inspiration, and my imagination turned the tables on me instead. I suppose there's a lesson here. One needs to control how imagination works or it will run wild.

Inspiration, however, may be derived by personal phenomena, an unfortunate childhood, abuse, tragedy, loss, unrequited love, health, etc. Some of my past health issues provided inspiration. As a pre-adolescent I had a bout of rheumatic fever. I remember my bed was encapsulated by a plastic tent. My parents became overly protective, removing me from normal child recreation outdoors and with friends. I remember rebelling, developing an attitude to prove I wasn't as vulnerable as they believed. That chip on my shoulder didn't dissipate over time. I became a fierce competitor in everything.

Another health issue was more profound. It led me to reinvent myself as an author. My wife drove me to the hospital because of chest discomfort. After a heart catheter I was prepped for a quintuple bypass. On the way to the O.R., my heart attack couldn't wait. The attendant's brisk pace turned into a full sprint, rushing me down a corridor. I remember thinking, *if I make it out of here alive I'm going to give up my law career and do the things that matter most*. High on the list was to begin that writing career I always wanted.

Waking up with my breastbone sawed down the middle from stem to stern, then cracked open like a lobster before the eating begins, left another impression on me. It turned my intention to write into a life and death commitment. In the recovery room with my wife, my daughter, and my best friend, I told them about my new ambition. I was asked, "How are you going to do this?" I don't remember my exact reply, but I had been preparing for this my entire law career. I encountered so many interesting characters, scoundrels and heroes, and the unbelievable predicaments they managed to get in. I committed them to memory, hoping I would find the opportunity to write novels.

Writer's block would not be a concern for me. I had so many things to write about. And because of my experiences, I could revel in my vulnerability. After my first two novels, I realized that I must open my soul further, like the heart surgeon who had opened my chest, revealing the damage and hurt, allowing my heart to enter the story and pump emotion into every thought.

Trust me, that's a hard thing to do, let alone sustain over a long period of time. I was opening my emotions in spurts in my first two novels. Then a fellow author who read my second book said, "You grabbed me here and there, but it's wasn't enough. I wanted to remain emotionally chained to the story. Give me more of a raw experience."

I asked, "How do I do that?"

"Only you can answer that," he responded.

That's what all novelists are searching for. It's the holy grail of writing. If we can tap into an inspiration and keep the candle burning brightly, to warm a heart or illuminate the pain of injustice, we will be a success. And if we're lucky, we might provide a moment or a memory that entertains the reader and enriches a life.

I'm fortunate I still have inspirations. I don't take them lightly. Thus, I return to my apology. If you notice me looking at you in a different way, or if I say something out of character, I might be looking for a new inspiration. Indulge me – I'm a writer.

The Spore Family
John Sheffield

There was a policeman called Spore
Who chased ne'er-do-wells by the score.
All were caught by this man,
Who was inside each plan.
For no one is outside the law.

There was a general named Spore
Who longed for war more and more.
He said, "If hostilities cease,
I'll soon wreck the peace,
And reestablish military law."

There was a scientist, Doctor Spore,
A famous and praised inventor.
He said, "I perceive
That problems, lesser men leave,
May be solved using Spore's general law."

There was an old fellow named Spore,
Who was an incredible bore.
He'd chatter and chatter
About now't that did matter.
So they threw him right out of the door.

A physician, the mad Doctor Spore,
Shocked patients right to the core.
He said, "If you want my aid,
Then after I'm paid,
Your health I guarantee to restore."

There once was a starlet named Spore,
Vivacious and full of glamour.
She said, "While my tits
Are outstanding bits,
They're not all that some have eyes for."

There was a grocer called Spore
Who became quite a bore, for
He talked nothing but shop,

And said, "I'm sure to be top.
By that I set great store."

An explorer, Sir Justinian Spore
Was lost up on bleak Bodmin Moor.
They searched and they saw
Him stuck high on a tor,
And they laughed, for he'd been stuck there before.

There once was a huntsman called Spore,
Who careered around chasing the boar
That he hoped to devour.
But one caught him and tore
His pants, which caused quite a furor.

Damn Marching Bands
John Sheffield

I was walking down the high street with my honey,
Feeling loose and kinda cool just holding hands.
When she let go and started moving to the music.
It was one of those damned marching bands.

Now, the sound of distant drumming should have warned me.
The tympanies like insistent falling rain.
Now she's following the trombones and the trumpets,
And I'll never see my sweetheart again.

I heard she had been seen in Austin, Texas,
A place that I had once called my home.
But by the time I reached there she had moved on.
And from now on all she'll ever do is roam.

So if you hear the sound of distant drumming,
Remember you have something bad to fear.
Grab your sweetie by the arm and start running.
You'd be smart to get the hell right out of there.

I Believe in Failure

Megan Benoit Ratcliff

I believe in failure. I believe in losing games, getting an "F," burning toast, and collecting rejection letters. I believe in failure because expecting perfection is unrealistic and ultimately counterproductive to living a bold life. When someone fails, they have, at the very least, put themselves out there in an attempt to do something meaningful or different than what they had been doing. When someone fears failure, they lock the door of opportunity and hide underneath the safety blanket of a boring, predictable life.

"There is no failure, just unfinished success." The quip from the radio host was intended to be encouraging, a pat on the back for those experiencing acute disappointment or a big soft hug for those with chronic low self-esteem. It aligns with the philosophy that everyone who plays deserves a trophy, everyone who shows up gets an "A," and everyone earns the same year-end bonus regardless of his or her productivity. My 6-year old son sitting in the back seat on his way to hockey practice doesn't need to hear that message. He would benefit from hearing the truth: failure is a part of life. No one is perfect. The only person who never fails is the person who never tries.

Not that I am making a case for mediocrity, low ambition and laziness. Failure comes in many forms, some more laudable than others. The lack-of-effort-and-preparation failure is not of what I write. I have had more than enough of these self-destructions: a graduation speech that I jotted down in the 11th hour and didn't rehearse; training that I didn't do before trying out for the college soccer team; not attending the funeral of a good friend's husband. These failures are not always relegated to laziness, selfishness, or social ineptitude, though they can be. In some instances, they are driven by subconscious self-sabotage, the voice in our brain that whispers "you are not enough." Sometimes it is easier to not put in effort and write off one's failings with a blasé "I didn't really care" than it is to put in one's best effort and admit that it wasn't enough. These lack-of-effort failures can be redeemed when they are thoughtfully contemplated and used as an impetus for growth.

And then there are the tried-hard-but-didn't-make it failures. These are the ones to be lauded.

Failing takes courage and it takes knowing that what we do and how we perform does not define who we are. Failing builds character. Michael Jordan, arguably the best basketball player who ever played, mused in a 2012 ad, "I've missed more than 9,000 shots in my career, I've lost almost 300 games. Twenty-six times I've been trusted to take the game winning shot…and missed. I've lost over and over and over again in my life, and that is why I succeed." Failure met with perseverance is another word for practice.

Failure needs to be re-conceptualized in our societal psyche as an acceptable part of the process of becoming. Our achievement-oriented focus on success at any cost is creating a generation of overly anxious, color-inside-the-lines, approval-seeking, teach-to-the-test children who look great on paper but who are afraid to think or live outside the box. In his book, *Excellent Sheep: The Miseducation of the American Elite and the Way to a Meaningful Life* William Deresiewicz writes: "The system manufactures students who are smart and talented and driven, yes, but also anxious, timid, and lost, with little intellectual curiosity and a stunted sense of purpose: trapped in a bubble of privilege, heading meekly in the same direction, great at what they're doing but with no idea why they're doing it." We were not designed to be lemmings, we were designed for free will. This is necessarily a non-linear process fraught with miscalculation, course corrections and trepidation. It in an expedition into unknown waters, the rewards of which are innumerable if we can muster the courage to haul anchor and go.

I have experienced innumerable failures in my own life. Acts of commission and acts of omission; both have shaped me. From perceived failures, however, have come some of my most courageous victories: overcoming an eating disorder that was slowly, insidiously taking over my life; learning to swim just prior to my 30th birthday after living my early years deathly afraid of water; graduating magna cum laude from college after not being elected into the National Honor Society in high school; writing in the public domain after years of putting it off in pursuit of more practical pursuits. There is no failure except that dream or conviction of heart that is left unrealized.

Failure teaches us that we still have a lot to learn. It teaches us that we have the capacity for perseverance, strength, and ingenuity beyond our imagination. Failure teaches us humility and grace, not only for ourselves, but for others as well. When we are less afraid to fail, we are more likely to aspire to great things. That aspiration is what I want for my son, careening into the hockey net head first after a missed shot. Keep shooting, son, and you will score. As Wayne Gretzky said, "You miss 100% of the shots you never take."

Maybe It's About the Story

Megan Benoit Ratcliff

Maybe it's not about the happy ending, maybe it's about the story.

Athena Orchard from Leicester, England wrote the above words at the age of 13 while undergoing treatment for osteosarcoma (bone cancer). Her words were prophetic; she died May 28, 2014 less than 6 months after her initial diagnosis.

The truth of Athena's story is that we all are living on borrowed time in stories partly constructed by our own devices and partly by the world around us. No one knows the number of their days or what fate might befall them. I have often wondered if knowing the date of my demise would inspire me to live more fully each day or if it would fill me with grief, dread, or apathy so strong I would retreat from living, white flag of surrender raised. Ultimately the question is irrelevant. Ten days or forty-seven years; length doesn't matter. Time is the only commodity that is truly priceless. Time can't be hoarded. There is no saving up for a rainy day. Every day is an investment: 1,440 minutes. Binge watching Game of Thrones or playing Candy Crush comes at a calculable cost, the benefit of which is highly subjective. We need to decide for ourselves: what is an investment and what is a waste?

True appreciation of time is rare. More often than not we are just trying to get through: how many days until the weekend/vacation/semesters end/paycheck? Even faced with imminent death, time seems to slip away, days into weeks into months filtered through a meaning-seeking sieve. I experienced third-hand the slow death of my writing partner's life partner. He was diagnosed with stage IV prostate cancer in 2010 and given 9-12 months to live. Intensive medical treatment and a persistent (read: stubborn) personality yielded an additional 2 years.

What was the value of that time? Only Joe could say. Undoubtedly there were many doldrums days filled with doctor appointments, "putting affairs in order," and tolerating discomfort associated with medication side effects and disease progression. But outside of the chronological day-to-day passage of time ("chronos" in ancient Greek) were priceless "kairos" moments: seeing his son marry, watching the ocean's tide one last time in Punta Gorda, one last dance and tender embrace with Peg. Those moments, outside of the monotony of every day, laden with meaning and beauty, are what make any life worth living and any story worth telling. Perhaps in valuing time we can cultivate more of those moments in our every day, ending be damned. A lingering embrace; a long overdue call to a friend; appreciating the seasonal shift of nature outside our window. Moments outside of time occur when we open ourselves to them.

So maybe it IS about the story. Maybe how we choose to live our lives (the big picture) and how we spend the minutes in our days (the pixels) determines whether our stories are dime store dramas or epic tales. I, personally, am in pursuit of the latter. An imperfect heroine pursuing something consequential, a mission to impact the world in some way for someone for some net gain other than my own bottom line. I want to make connections, take chances, dream big, laugh often, and sleep soundly without regret knowing that, as much as I could, I wrote my story instead of waiting for it to be written around me. The last sentence be what it may, but until then, give me the pen. Joe had 74 years. Athena had 13. How many will you have? God only knows. The more important questions is: how will you invest the borrowed time you have into the story you are creating?

Biographies

Marty Aftewicz has writing credits, which include numerous freelance magazine articles, a non-fiction Internet Marketing book, and writing contributions to a children's book which targeted a non-profit organization dedicated to fostering young adults' interest in aviation. In 2010, I received an award as Master of Excellence for Commitment to the Community in Atlanta. Most notably, I am a past president and now serve as Officer Emeritus for The Atlanta Writers Club, one of the largest, oldest, and most active writing organizations in the United States.

Valerie Joan Connors arrived in Atlanta in 1996, the same day as the Olympic torch. Born in the Upper Peninsula of Michigan, Valerie's family moved her out west, where she spent her formative years in Eugene, Oregon. She then bounced up and down the west coast, spending time in San Diego, Seattle, and Portland, before her job as a software consultant brought her to Georgia. Valerie is the author of four novels, *In Her Keeping, Shadow of a Smile, A Promise Made*, and her latest, *A Better Truth.* She credits her association with the Atlanta Writers Club for the fact that her four novels have been both written and published. She has happily served on the AWC Board since 2011 in nearly every capacity, including as President from 2013 to 2015. She continues to serve as the VP of Programming and Officer Emerita. During business hours, Valerie is the CFO of an engineering firm. She is a dog person, and supports big cat conservation by accredited sanctuaries. Valerie lives in Norcross with her husband and two dogs, and is working on her next novel.

Susan Crawford is the author of *The Pocket Wife* and *The Other Widow* (Morrow-Harper Collins), Susan grew up in Miami, Florida and graduated from the University of Miami with a B.A. in English and a Minor in Psychology. She later moved to New York City and then to Boston before settling in Atlanta to raise three daughters and to work in the field of Adult Education. A member of The Atlanta Writers Club and The Village Writers, Susan lives with her husband and a trio of rescue cats.

Tom Leidy's career in academe – teaching psychology, statistics, and research design – was interrupted when he moved south to do marketing research – first with a little-known but highly regarded beverage firm; later with a major manufacturer of family apparel and underwear. His interest in writing evolved after he returned south after completing assignments in Europe, Japan and Australia. To date, his output includes three novels and several short stories – all set in Ohio; none yet published.

Jeremy Logan is the pen name of a writer of mystery/suspense novels. Born in Ohio, he attended high school, college and law school in Georgia. He has resided in metro Atlanta since 1966. He retired from his legal career in 2008, to begin to do what he always wanted to do, write novels. His legal career specialized in disaster response in the transportation and oil industry. Married forty-three years, and has one child, Jeremy's first novel was self-published, and his two latest were published by Deeds Publishing. His most recent, ***SMITTEN***, was launched this year. He describes *Smitten* as "*A coming of age romance interrupted by a serial killer*". It's based on his experience with a high school classmate that became one of Georgia's most notorious serial killers.

Susan J McBreairty, a Mainer, grew up wanting to discover the world far away from her wilderness home. She accomplished that early in life through reading. She loaded up with inspiration when the Bookmobile came to her school. With a sense of adventure, always, she's lived several times in the Deep South; the Pacific Northwest; lived in Sweden and traveled throughout Scandinavia, as well as England, Scotland, and Ireland. She turned 50 years old in the United States Peace Corps where she served in Craiova, Romania. Susan hopes her short stories, and eventual novels, will speak to the reader's heart and stir emotions of love, hate, fear, and adventure.

Chris Negron graduated from Yale University, where he wrote sports for the nation's oldest daily college newspaper, the Yale Daily News. His short fiction has previously appeared in WhiskeyPaper, Pithead Chapel, Spilled Milk Magazine, The Vignette Review, The Grand Central Review, and elsewhere. His story "The Pipe Bomb", which appeared in Split Lip Magazine, was longlisted for wigleaf.com's Top 50 (very) Short Stories of 2015. He currently lives in Atlanta with his wife and can usually be found in some coffee shop working on his first novel or another short story. Learn more at chrisnegron.com.

Richard Perreault, a native of Atlanta, now lives in Bryson City, North Carolina on a mountaintop overlooking the Great Smoky Mountain National Park. Since turning his writing focus to short fiction in 2011, Richard's stories have won more than 30 awards. All proceeds from the sale of his book, *Toto Too – The True Story of What Happened Over the Rainbow*, the Wizard of Oz story told from Toto's point of view, have been donated to animal rescue shelters.

Clayton H Ramsey is a former two-term president of the Atlanta Writers Club who remains on the Board as an Officer Emeritus. He has served as a panel moderator at the Decatur Book Festival, a reader for the Townsend Prize for Fiction, and a freelance editor and speechwriter. He is the co-author of a number of scientific papers and his fiction has been recognized by the AWC, the Georgia Writers Museum, and Mash Stories. He and his wife live in Decatur, Georgia.

Megan Benoit Ratcliff is a Yankee-born, moderately introverted, mother of two great kids who totally turned her life upside down following their conception. Trained as a clinical pediatric psychologist, she got off the proverbial hamster wheel when she realized she wasn't following the advice she was giving to families on how to live purposefully. A closet writer since age 11 (with several letters to the editor and magazine reviews to her credit), she is working on her first nonfiction book about family thriving. She aspires to not be a hypocrite.

Carolyn Robbins has written several books, including *Caribbean Green*, and also has had magazine articles published. A collection of children stories is gathering dust waiting to get published also exist. She attended both Northern Illinois University and Northwestern University and now lives in Marietta with her husband. She spends time keeping track of her six grandchildren, gardens, and meets once a week with fellow authors to discuss their manuscripts.

Dr. Terry Segal earned a Ph.D. in Energy Medicine, M.A. in Educational Psychology and M.A. in Theatre Arts. A licensed psychotherapist for nearly 30 years, she authored the self-help book **The EnchantedJourney: Finding the Key That Unlocks You** and **Hidden Corners of My Heart**, a contemporary women's fiction novel. Terry's poetry and prose have been published, along with a monthly New Moon Meditations column for the Atlanta Jewish Times. Her weekly Enchanted Blog is in its sixth year. Four of her plays were performed at the Atlanta One-Minute Play Festival. Dr. Segal is also a public speaker and mixed media artist. Her mission: "To banish stress and transform life into an enchanted journey" through compassion, humor and Ten Enchanted Keys, which include journaling, meditation, art, movement and connection to nature. She inspires others to battle their Dragons of Stress and feel empowered to create life as they wish it were. Enchanted Journey online courses will reach wider audiences. The more tranquil people are the better off the world will be. Terry is also a union actress in SAG/AFTRA/AEA. www.DrTerrySegal.com.

Brenda Sevcik grew up in Minnesota, but has resided in Milton, Georgia for nearly twenty years. When Rachel, her youngest child, left home for college, she gave Brenda a wooden plaque that read, "Try". Rachel, knowing her mother needed to tell her stories of the complexity of the human spirit along with the power of unconditional acceptance and forgiveness, urged Brenda to begin writing them down. *Different Colors* is Brenda's debut publication.

John Sheffield is a physicist who has been writing for many decades. Among his recent publications are: *Plasma Scattering of Electromagnetic Radiation,* Elsevier 2011,and a humorous memoir, *Fun in Fusion Research,* Elsevier 2013—the subject of talks at DragonCon in 2013 and 2014—and a mystery novel, *Roseland's Secret,* Deeds Publishing 2015. A sequel, *Return to Roseland,* was published in August 2016. He is fortunate to be a member of the Atlanta Writers Club, where he has won two first place prizes for poetry. In 2015, he won the Southeastern Writers Association's Edna Sampson Award for an unpublished novel *My Friend Albert.* He lives in Woodstock with his wife Sharon and three cats. http://john-sheffield-author.com

Jan Slimming was born and educated in London, England. After college she soon found herself in the British book publishing industry, from which she never looked back. Following a successful career in production, foreign rights and international sales, for more than twenty years, she now finds herself as an author on the other side of the key-board, in an interesting role reversal. This anthology extract is her first publication and a precursor to her memoir and history of her mother, Daisy Lawrence—a Bletchley Park Codebreaker during World War II— soon to be published. Jan lives in Atlanta, GA, with her husband and three college-age children.

John Tabellione, a former sales and marketing executive with Fortune 500 firms, is an award-winnning, professional freelance business writer in Atlanta. He creates content for multiple websites, brochures, case studies, press releases and newsletters. His recent travel memoir about serendipitous driving adventures in Italy is entitled, *Pit Stops, Pitfalls & Olive Pits*, and he is researching another tourism book.Tabellione has also produced hundreds of creative posts since 2010 on his blog, "Tabs on Writing," which provides a light-hearted approach to grammar, punctuation, spelling, homophones, and word derivations, weaving grammatical advice through anecdotal news stories from past and present. He has published feature articles in the following magazines: *Georgia Backroads; LaSalette America; Applicator; Expectant Mother's Guide; and Welcome.* He is a contributing writer to EastCobber.com, a local news website, and his work has appeared in LikeThe Dew.com, a news, opinion and culture site. Tabellione is a member of the Atlanta Writers Club, the Northpoint Writers' Critique Group and the Knights of Columbus, and is a U.S. Air Force veteran.

Jane Turner-Haessler is an American born Brit, forced to drink PG Tips and eat boiled puddings by her British parents. She is a painter first, writer second. She has lived all over the world and many of her stories reflect her strange childhood. She has been a member of The Atlanta Writers Group for five years, hosting monthly critique groups at her house. Her Short stories have been published on several online publications. She is working on her third novel, trying this time to write something lighter, deciding to let the main characters live.

George Weinstein is the author of the mystery novel *Aftermath* (published in October 2016), the modern romance novel *The Caretaker*, the Southern historical novel *Hardscrabble Road* and the multi-cultural historical novel *The Five Destinies of Carlos Moreno*. His work has been published locally in the Atlanta press and in regional and national anthologies, including *A Cup of Comfort for Writers*. His first novel, the children's motivational adventure *Jake and the Tiger Flight*, was written for the nonprofit Tiger Flight Foundation, which is dedicated to the mission of leading the young to become the "Pilot in Command" of their lives. George is the former President of and has been an active participant in the Atlanta Writers Club since 2000. Information about George and his books is available on his website: www.GeorgeWeinstein.com.

Mary Wivell lives and writes in Atlanta, Georgia. She holds a B.A. in fiction writing from the University of Pittsburgh. She has previously published short fiction in *The Medulla Review*. When she's not writing, gardening or bird-watching, she's attending the needs of three persnickety felines and fifteen persistently blooming orchids.

Lisa Youngblood recently left Atlanta for the mountains of North Carolina, where the only sounds at night come from turkeys, frogs and thunder. Her stories have been accepted for publication in *REAL: Regarding Arts & Letters, Confluence, Talking River, Portland Review, Porcupine Magazine and The Rambler*. She attended the Sewanee Writers Conference in 2010 and The Narrative Writer's Workshop in 2011. She is currently seeking a home for her novel THE MAGIC MULE. She is a member of The Atlanta Writers' Club and the Village Writers' Group and has worked in critique groups with both.